I0012647

Advanced Integration Techniques

Cross-Platform Application Development with Python and C# for Enterprise-Grade Solutions

THOMPSON CARTER

All rights reserved

No part of this book may be reproduced, distributed, or transmitted in any form or by any means without the prior written permission of the publisher, except in the case of brief quotations embodied in critical reviews and certain other noncommercial uses permitted by right law.

Table of Content

TABLE OF CONTENTS

Introduction

Building Cross-Platform Solutions: Leveraging Python and C# for Scalable, Secure, and Agile Applications

In today's rapidly evolving software development landscape, the need for cross-platform applications has never been more pronounced. Organizations, from small startups to large enterprises, are increasingly facing the challenge of delivering seamless, consistent user experiences across a variety of devices and platforms. Whether it's a mobile application that needs to work on both iOS and Android, or a web application that should function smoothly across all modern browsers, the demand for cross-platform development is a driving force in modern software engineering.

This book, *Building Cross-Platform Solutions: Leveraging Python and C# for Scalable, Secure, and Agile Applications*, is designed to provide developers with the knowledge and tools necessary to build efficient, scalable, and secure cross-platform applications using two of the most powerful programming languages in the industry: Python and C#. Both Python and C# have carved out their places in the development ecosystem, offering unique strengths that, when combined, enable developers to create robust solutions that can run seamlessly across a variety of platforms.

The goal of this book is to not only guide you through the technical aspects of building cross-platform applications but also to help you understand the principles, challenges, and best practices that come with developing in today's heterogeneous computing environments.

Why Cross-Platform Development?

In the past, developing software meant committing to a specific platform. If you wanted to create an application for Windows, you would write your code using Windows-specific technologies. Similarly, if you wanted to build a mobile app, you would write it using iOS-specific or Android-specific tools and languages. However, this approach can be inefficient, costly, and time-consuming. The need to develop and maintain separate codebases for each platform often results in duplicated effort, inconsistencies across platforms, and long development cycles.

Cross-platform development eliminates these issues by allowing developers to create applications that can run on multiple platforms using a single codebase. This approach is not only cost-effective but also ensures that users have a consistent experience, whether they are accessing the app on a desktop, tablet, or smartphone.

Python and **C#** are two of the most widely used programming languages that lend themselves well to cross-platform development, and each brings its own set of strengths. Python's simplicity, flexibility, and rich ecosystem make it a great choice for backend services, automation, data analysis, and machine learning tasks. C#, on the other hand, is a powerful language with strong support for building enterprise-grade applications, particularly in the Microsoft ecosystem, and it plays a key role in cross-platform mobile and desktop development through **Xamarin** and **.NET Core**.

What You Will Learn

Throughout this book, we'll explore how to leverage both Python and C# to build scalable, secure, and agile cross-platform applications. The structure of the book is designed to gradually build your expertise, from understanding the fundamental principles of cross-platform development to mastering advanced integration techniques and best practices.

Key concepts covered in this book include:

- **Foundations of Cross-Platform Development**: Learn the principles of building applications that can run seamlessly across multiple platforms, from mobile devices to desktops and web browsers.
- **Frameworks and Tools for Cross-Platform Development**: Discover powerful frameworks like **Xamarin**, **Flutter**, **Electron**, **React Native**, and how to integrate Python and C# into these frameworks for maximum flexibility.
- **Building APIs for Cross-Platform Communication**: Understand how to design and implement APIs that allow different parts of your application to communicate across various platforms. You'll learn how to use RESTful APIs, WebSockets, and messaging queues.
- **UI/UX Consistency**: Explore strategies for ensuring your user interfaces (UIs) are responsive, consistent, and adaptable across different screen sizes and devices, using tools like **Xamarin.Forms**, **React**, and **PyQt**.
- **Testing, Debugging, and Performance Optimization**: Dive into testing strategies that ensure your cross-platform application performs optimally across all

environments, and learn how to debug issues that arise from platform-specific differences.

- **Integration with Legacy Systems**: Discover strategies for integrating modern cross-platform applications with existing enterprise systems, including the use of middleware, messaging queues, and service-oriented architecture (SOA).
- **Security and Scalability Best Practices**: Learn how to build secure and scalable cross-platform applications by implementing robust authentication, authorization, and data management practices.

Real-World Examples and Case Studies

One of the key strengths of this book is the inclusion of **real-world case studies** that showcase how companies have successfully leveraged Python and C# for cross-platform development. These case studies highlight the challenges developers face when building cross-platform applications and how they overcame them using the techniques and tools discussed in the book.

From integrating legacy systems in the banking sector to building scalable cloud-based solutions for e-commerce platforms, these case studies offer valuable insights into how to approach cross-platform development in a business context. You'll see how Python and C# can be combined to create full-stack solutions that integrate backend services, frontend UIs, and third-party APIs.

Why Python and C#?

While there are many languages available for cross-platform development, Python and C# stand out for several reasons:

- **Python**: Known for its simplicity and ease of use, Python is widely adopted in fields such as data science, machine learning, web development, and backend services. Its vast library ecosystem and flexibility allow it to be used for building the backend of cross-platform applications, handling automation, data processing, and integration tasks.
- **C#**: A statically typed, object-oriented language developed by Microsoft, C# is widely used in building enterprise applications, particularly in environments like **.NET Core** and **Xamarin**. Its ability to work across platforms, combined with powerful frameworks like **.NET MAUI** and **Xamarin**, makes it an excellent choice for building cross-platform desktop, mobile, and cloud applications.

The combination of Python and C# in cross-platform development offers a powerful synergy: Python handles backend data processing and AI-driven services, while C# handles user-facing interfaces and enterprise-level solutions. Together, they provide a comprehensive stack for modern application development.

Why This Book is Important

As businesses increasingly demand applications that run seamlessly across various platforms and devices, cross-platform development has become an essential skill for developers. However, developing cross-platform applications is not without its challenges. This book aims to provide you with a comprehensive understanding of how to leverage Python and C# for building scalable, secure, and high-performance applications that can run on mobile, desktop, and web platforms.

By reading this book, you will gain practical knowledge and hands-on experience in building enterprise-grade cross-platform solutions. Whether you're a beginner who wants to get started with cross-platform development or an experienced developer looking to expand your skill set, this book will serve as your guide to mastering cross-platform application development using two of the most popular programming languages in the world.

Who This Book is For

This book is intended for:

- **Developers** who are interested in building cross-platform applications using Python and C#.
- **Enterprise architects** looking to modernize legacy systems and integrate them with new cross-platform solutions.
- **Mobile and web developers** who want to understand the intricacies of cross-platform development and learn best practices for building scalable applications.
- **Software engineers** who want to explore the potential of Python and C# in cross-platform application development and how to integrate them for enterprise solutions.

In conclusion, this book provides a deep dive into the world of cross-platform application development, leveraging the power of Python and C# to build scalable, secure, and agile solutions. The insights, case studies, and best practices shared here will help you navigate the challenges of modern software development and equip you with the tools needed to succeed in the cross-platform landscape.

CHAPTER 1

INTRODUCTION TO CROSS-PLATFORM DEVELOPMENT

Overview of Cross-Platform Development

Cross-platform development refers to the practice of creating software applications that can run on multiple operating systems or platforms without requiring separate codebases for each. In traditional software development, applications were often built specifically for one operating system—such as Windows, macOS, or Linux—resulting in the need to write different versions of the same application for each platform. Cross-platform development aims to eliminate this redundancy by using shared code that can be compiled and run on different environments.

The key benefit of this approach is efficiency. Developers can write the code once and deploy it across several platforms, drastically reducing the time, effort, and costs associated with maintaining multiple versions of an app. Cross-platform development frameworks, such as .NET Core for C# and various Python libraries (like Kivy or PyQt), enable this type of development by providing the necessary tools and abstraction layers for developers to write universal applications.

Importance in the Enterprise Context

In the enterprise environment, cross-platform development has become an essential strategy for organizations looking to expand their reach and improve operational efficiency. Enterprises need to cater to a broad range of devices, operating systems, and user environments, often with limited resources. By adopting a cross-platform development approach, businesses can reach users across various systems, whether it's desktop applications, mobile apps, or web-based solutions.

Enterprise software often needs to be deployed on different operating systems and devices, which increases the complexity of development and maintenance. Cross-platform frameworks help enterprises streamline the development process by offering a unified solution to support various platforms. With the growing trend toward hybrid cloud systems and mobile-first strategies, having a unified development environment is critical for ensuring that applications are accessible on any device or operating system.

Additionally, cross-platform development helps businesses save costs by minimizing the need for specialized developers and reducing the time-to-market for new features or updates. This ability to quickly adapt and maintain applications across various platforms is especially important in competitive industries.

Key Differences Between Python and C# in Cross-Platform Solutions

While Python and C# both offer powerful cross-platform capabilities, they do so in different ways. Understanding the nuances of each language is critical when deciding which to use for your project.

Python:

- **Flexibility and simplicity**: Python is known for its simplicity, readability, and rapid development capabilities. Its extensive collection of libraries and frameworks, such as Kivy, PyQt, and Flask, make it a go-to option for quick, scalable, and easy-to-maintain cross-platform applications.
- **Platform-independent runtime**: Python relies on an interpreter, which allows it to run on any platform with a Python runtime installed. However, some specific

features might not be as optimized across platforms, especially for complex, high-performance applications.

C#:

- **Enterprise-level support**: C# is primarily associated with the Microsoft ecosystem and has long been used to build Windows applications. However, with the introduction of .NET Core (now known as .NET 5+), C# has become a powerful cross-platform language, supporting not only Windows but also Linux and macOS. This makes it an excellent choice for enterprise-grade applications that require high performance, security, and scalability.

- **Rich IDE and tooling**: Visual Studio, the primary IDE for C#, offers robust support for cross-platform development with .NET Core. Its integration with Azure and various cloud services makes C# a strong contender for cloud-based, enterprise solutions.

Both Python and C# support multiple platforms, but the choice between them often depends on the specific needs of the application, the desired performance, and the existing technology stack within the enterprise.

Benefits and Challenges

Benefits:

1. **Cost Efficiency**: Cross-platform development allows companies to write and maintain a single codebase, which reduces costs associated with having separate teams or specialized developers for each platform.

2. **Faster Time-to-Market**: With shared codebases, businesses can quickly launch updates and new features across all supported platforms without delay, ensuring quicker releases and continuous improvement.

3. **Wider Reach**: Cross-platform apps enable businesses to reach a larger audience by supporting various platforms and devices. This is especially important in today's diverse ecosystem of operating systems, from mobile to desktop to cloud.

4. **Unified User Experience**: By using cross-platform tools and frameworks, developers can ensure that users across different platforms receive a consistent experience, which is critical for brand identity and user satisfaction.

Challenges:

1. **Performance Optimization**: Cross-platform solutions sometimes face performance issues when compared to native applications. The abstraction layer required to

make applications work across multiple platforms can lead to inefficiencies, particularly for performance-intensive applications.

2. **Limited Access to Platform-Specific Features**: While cross-platform frameworks offer a unified codebase, they may not support all the unique features of each platform. If an application relies on platform-specific functionality, the developer might face challenges in accessing those features.

3. **Compatibility Issues**: Despite being marketed as "cross-platform," there may still be minor bugs and issues when running the same application on different platforms. These issues typically arise from differences in how operating systems handle hardware, memory management, or system calls.

4. **Learning Curve**: While Python and C# are both relatively easy to learn individually, mastering how to integrate them in a cross-platform context—along with dealing with issues like debugging and platform-specific quirks—can be daunting for developers new to the ecosystem.

In this chapter, we've set the stage for understanding the landscape of cross-platform development. The subsequent chapters will dive deeper into specific tools, strategies, and best practices for creating enterprise-grade applications using Python and C#.

CHAPTER 2

THE EVOLUTION OF PYTHON AND C# FOR ENTERPRISE SOLUTIONS

Historical Perspective of Python and C#

Python: Python, created in the late 1980s by Guido van Rossum, has grown from a simple scripting language to one of the most widely-used programming languages in the world. Its journey began as a hobby project but quickly gained traction due to its simplicity and readability. By the 2000s, Python had become a powerful tool for various applications, ranging from web development to scientific computing.

While Python initially gained popularity in academia, data science, and scripting, it wasn't until the rise of open-source development and the increasing demand for automation that Python truly found its place in the enterprise world. The language's extensive libraries, ease of learning, and cross-platform capabilities have made it an attractive choice for building large-scale enterprise applications.

As Python matured, frameworks such as Django (for web development) and Flask (for microservices) solidified its standing as a practical tool for enterprise solutions. With the rise of machine learning and artificial intelligence, Python has further entrenched itself as the go-to language for AI applications, enabling enterprises to integrate cutting-edge technology into their operations.

C#: C# was developed by Microsoft in the early 2000s as part of its .NET framework. Initially, it was designed to compete with Java and offer a more modern, object-oriented alternative. C# quickly became a key part of the .NET ecosystem, which was predominantly focused on Windows development.

However, as the demand for cross-platform applications grew, Microsoft made a significant shift with the release of .NET Core in 2016, which allowed C# to be used beyond Windows. This transformation has made C# one of the most powerful and popular languages for building scalable, enterprise-grade applications across different platforms.

The evolution of C# has also been marked by continuous improvements, such as enhanced language features (e.g., LINQ, async/await), robust libraries, and integration with modern cloud platforms like Azure. C# is now seen as a versatile language that can handle everything from web development to enterprise-level systems and mobile applications.

Why These Languages Are Pivotal for Modern Enterprise Applications

Python's Role in Modern Enterprises:

1. **Simplicity and Rapid Development**: Python's clean, readable syntax and ease of use make it ideal for rapid application development, which is crucial for enterprises in today's fast-paced digital landscape. Businesses need to adapt quickly, and Python allows developers to build and deploy applications in a fraction of the time it might take with other languages.

2. **Versatility Across Domains**: Python's extensive ecosystem of libraries and frameworks allows it to be used in a wide range of applications, from web development and data analysis to machine learning and automation. This versatility is a huge advantage for enterprises that need to implement diverse solutions under one umbrella.

3. **Integration with Cutting-Edge Technologies**: Python is at the forefront of AI, machine learning, and big data analytics. For enterprises looking to leverage data science and AI for competitive advantage, Python is often the language of choice. Libraries like TensorFlow, Pandas, and PyTorch make it easy for businesses to integrate these technologies into their applications.

4. **Cross-Platform Support**: Python can run on Windows, Linux, and macOS, making it ideal for cross-platform development. Enterprises are increasingly choosing Python to build solutions that work across different systems and devices, reducing the need for separate development teams for each platform.

C#'s Role in Modern Enterprises:

1. **Enterprise-Grade Performance**: C# is a high-performance language that is well-suited for large-scale enterprise applications. With the optimization capabilities of .NET Core and the robust support for multi-threading, C# can handle the heavy lifting required by enterprise-grade software, especially

24

when it comes to handling complex business logic, large volumes of data, and high traffic.

2. **Ecosystem and Tooling**: The integration of C# with the .NET ecosystem offers enterprises access to powerful tools and frameworks, such as ASP.NET for web development and Entity Framework for database management. The robust Visual Studio IDE enhances developer productivity with advanced debugging, testing, and performance analysis tools.

3. **Cloud Integration and Scalability**: C# and .NET Core are tightly integrated with cloud platforms, particularly Microsoft Azure. Enterprises can build scalable, cloud-native applications with ease, benefiting from features like automatic scaling, robust security, and global deployment capabilities.

4. **Cross-Platform Development with .NET Core**: The introduction of .NET Core has allowed C# to transcend its Windows-only origins, making it an excellent choice for businesses looking to develop applications that run on Linux and macOS as well. This cross-platform capability is especially valuable for enterprises looking to deploy applications across different environments.

Industry Use Cases and Success Stories

Python:

1. **Data Analytics in Retail**: A global retail chain implemented a Python-based solution to analyze customer purchasing patterns and optimize inventory management. Using machine learning libraries like Scikit-learn and Pandas, the company was able to predict trends, adjust stock levels, and improve customer satisfaction. This integration of AI and data analytics allowed them to make data-driven decisions, ultimately increasing revenue and reducing waste.

2. **Financial Services and Risk Management**: A financial services firm used Python to build a real-time risk management system that could monitor global financial markets. By using Python's libraries for statistical analysis and financial modeling, the firm was able to predict market fluctuations and respond to changes in real time, saving millions of dollars in potential losses.

3. **Automation in Healthcare**: A healthcare provider utilized Python for automating medical record processing and streamlining administrative tasks.

Python's libraries for natural language processing (NLP) helped the organization quickly parse and categorize large volumes of medical data, improving both efficiency and accuracy in patient care.

C#:

1. **Enterprise Resource Planning (ERP) System**: A leading manufacturing company implemented an enterprise-wide ERP system built with C# and .NET Core. The solution enabled seamless integration of various business operations, such as finance, HR, and supply chain management, improving decision-making and reducing operational costs. C# provided the performance needed to handle real-time processing of critical data while ensuring scalability as the company grew.

2. **E-Commerce Platform**: An e-commerce giant turned to C# and ASP.NET Core to build a high-performance online shopping platform capable of handling millions of users and transactions. With C#'s speed and scalability, the platform could manage peak shopping periods without performance degradation, ensuring an optimal user experience.

3. **Cloud-based Healthcare System**: A healthcare organization adopted C# and .NET Core to create a cloud-based solution for managing patient records and treatment plans. The integration with Microsoft Azure allowed for easy scaling and secure storage of sensitive health data, while C#'s enterprise capabilities ensured the system could meet stringent healthcare regulations.

In this chapter, we've explored the historical development of Python and C# and why these languages are so pivotal for enterprise applications today. From Python's simplicity and adaptability to C#'s power and enterprise-grade features, both languages have proven themselves essential tools for building scalable, efficient, and robust applications in modern enterprises. The use cases highlighted here show just how far these technologies have come and how businesses can leverage them to stay competitive in the digital age.

CHAPTER 3

SETTING UP YOUR CROSS-PLATFORM DEVELOPMENT ENVIRONMENT

In this chapter, we'll cover the essential steps to get your development environment ready for cross-platform application development using Python and C#. We'll focus on installing and configuring Python, C#, and .NET Core, as well as setting up the integrated development environments (IDEs) for both languages. Additionally, we'll explore version control systems, particularly Git, which will help you manage your code across different platforms and teams.

Installing and Configuring Python, C#, and .NET Core

Python Installation: Python is relatively easy to install across platforms, and there are multiple methods to do so depending on your operating system.

1. **Windows**:
    o   Visit the official Python website.

- o Download the latest stable version of Python for Windows.
- o During installation, make sure to check the option that says **"Add Python to PATH"**. This step ensures that Python is accessible from the command line.
- o To verify installation, open Command Prompt and type `python --version`. If the version number shows up, Python is successfully installed.

2. **macOS**:

- o Python comes pre-installed on macOS. However, it's often an outdated version. To install the latest version, use a package manager like Homebrew.
- o Open Terminal and type `brew install python`. Once installed, verify with `python3 --version`.

3. **Linux**:

- o Python is typically pre-installed on most Linux distributions. To install or upgrade Python, use the following commands depending on your distribution:
    - **Debian/Ubuntu**: `sudo apt-get install python3`
    - **Fedora**: `sudo dnf install python3`
- o Verify with `python3 --version`.

C# and .NET Core Installation: C# is part of the .NET ecosystem, and with .NET Core, it can run across platforms (Windows, macOS, and Linux). Here's how you can install and set up .NET Core on your system:

1. **Windows**:
   - Download the latest version of .NET Core from the official .NET website.
   - Run the installer and follow the instructions.
   - To verify installation, open Command Prompt and type `dotnet --version`. If the version is displayed, it means .NET Core is installed correctly.

2. **macOS**:
   - To install .NET Core on macOS, use Homebrew by running: `brew install --cask dotnet-sdk`.
   - Verify the installation with `dotnet --version`.

3. **Linux**:
   - On Linux, install .NET Core through the package manager. For example:
     - **Ubuntu**: `sudo apt install dotnet-sdk-5.0`
     - **Fedora**: `sudo dnf install dotnet-sdk-5.0`

o   Check the installation with `dotnet --version`.

IDE and Tools Setup for Both Languages

Visual Studio for C#: Visual Studio is the most popular IDE for C# development, especially for .NET Core. It's feature-rich and designed to support large-scale enterprise applications, with strong support for debugging, testing, and performance profiling.

1. **Installation**:
   o   Download the latest version of Visual Studio from the official website.
   o   During installation, select the **".NET desktop development"** workload to ensure you have the tools needed for C# and .NET Core development.
2. **Key Features**:
   o   **IntelliSense**: Visual Studio offers IntelliSense, which provides code suggestions, parameter info, and quick documentation.
   o   **Debugger**: Visual Studio comes with a powerful debugger that helps you track down issues across platforms.
   o   **Version Control Integration**: Visual Studio supports Git out of the box, allowing you to manage your repositories directly within the IDE.

PyCharm for Python: PyCharm is one of the best IDEs for Python development, offering intelligent code completion, debugging tools, and excellent support for Python's vast array of libraries.

1. **Installation**:
   o Download PyCharm from the official JetBrains website.
   o There are two versions: **Community** (free) and **Professional** (paid). The Community version offers everything you need for most Python development.
   o Follow the installer instructions for your platform, and once installed, launch PyCharm.

2. **Key Features**:
   o **Code Completion**: PyCharm helps you write Python code more efficiently with context-aware suggestions.
   o **Debugging**: PyCharm provides a powerful debugging tool for stepping through your code and analyzing variable states.
   o **Virtual Environments**: PyCharm supports Python virtual environments, which is important for managing dependencies in Python projects.

Other Tools: While Visual Studio and PyCharm are the main IDEs, there are additional tools that can aid in cross-platform development:

- **Docker**: Containerization tool that ensures consistency across environments. You can create Docker containers for both Python and C# applications and run them on any platform.
- **Azure DevOps or GitHub Actions**: These CI/CD tools are integrated with Visual Studio and PyCharm, enabling automatic build and deployment of your cross-platform apps.
- **Postman**: A tool for testing and debugging APIs, particularly useful when building RESTful services with Python or C#.

Introduction to Version Control Systems (Git)

What is Version Control? Version control is a system that allows developers to track and manage changes to their codebase over time. It ensures that different versions of the code can be preserved and compared, making collaboration easier and safer. The most commonly used version control system today is **Git**, which allows developers to create and manage repositories of code.

Git Basics:

1. **Installation**:
   - ○ **Windows**: Download Git from the official Git website.
   - ○ **macOS**: Install Git using Homebrew with `brew install git`.
   - ○ **Linux**: Install Git via the terminal:
     - ▪ **Ubuntu**: `sudo apt-get install git`
     - ▪ **Fedora**: `sudo dnf install git`

2. **Setting Up Git**:
   - ○ Once installed, configure your Git identity using the following commands:

     ```bash
     Copy
     git config --global user.name "Your Name"
     git config --global user.email "youremail@example.com"
     ```

   - ○ This step ensures your commits are attributed to you.

3. **Basic Commands**:
   - ○ **Initialize a Repository**: `git init` – Initializes a new Git repository.

35

- o **Clone a Repository**: `git clone <repository_url>` – Clones an existing repository to your local machine.
- o **Staging Changes**: `git add <file>` – Adds a file to the staging area before committing.
- o **Commit Changes**: `git commit -m "Your commit message"` – Saves your changes to the repository with a message describing the changes.
- o **Push Changes**: `git push origin <branch>` – Pushes your changes to the remote repository.

4. **Branching and Merging**:
   - o **Create a New Branch**: `git branch <branch_name>` – Creates a new branch for features or bug fixes.
   - o **Switch Branches**: `git checkout <branch_name>` – Switches to another branch.
   - o **Merge Branches**: `git merge <branch_name>` – Merges changes from one branch into another.

Version Control in Team Environments: In team-based development, Git is crucial for collaboration. Teams use services like GitHub, GitLab, or Bitbucket to host their Git repositories in the cloud. These services offer additional tools like pull requests, issue tracking, and code reviews, which help teams collaborate and maintain high-quality code.

In this chapter, we've covered the installation and configuration of Python, C#, and .NET Core, as well as setting up IDEs like Visual Studio and PyCharm. We also introduced Git as a version control system that will help you manage your code and collaborate effectively in cross-platform development. With these tools in place, you are now ready to start building robust and scalable cross-platform applications!

CHAPTER 4

ARCHITECTURE FOR CROSS-PLATFORM SOLUTIONS

When developing cross-platform solutions, the architecture plays a crucial role in shaping the application's performance, scalability, and maintainability. In this chapter, we will explore how to choose the right architecture for your enterprise application, compare monolithic and microservices architectures, and discuss how to design scalable and maintainable solutions that can grow and adapt as your business needs evolve.

Choosing the Right Architecture for Enterprise Applications

Selecting the right architecture for your application depends on several factors, including the size and complexity of the project, the team's expertise, the need for scalability, and the long-term maintenance goals. An enterprise-grade solution must be able to handle high traffic loads, frequent updates, and seamless integration with other systems, all while maintaining reliability and performance.

There are two primary architectural models for building large-scale cross-platform applications:

1. **Monolithic Architecture**:

   o A monolithic architecture involves building the entire application as a single, unified codebase. All components—such as the front-end, back-end, and database—are tightly integrated into one system.

   o Monolithic applications are easier to develop initially and often require fewer resources for small teams or projects. They are ideal for applications that don't require frequent updates or extensive scalability in the early stages.

   When to Use Monolithic Architecture:

   o **Small to Medium-Sized Applications**: Monolithic architectures are suitable for applications where scalability is not a primary concern or where the application will remain relatively simple.

   o **Tightly Integrated Components**: If the components of your application are heavily interdependent and share a lot of data, a monolithic approach might be easier to implement and manage.

- o **Faster Development**: Since all parts of the application are built together, development is generally faster for monolithic solutions.

2. **Microservices Architecture**:

- o Microservices involve breaking down the application into smaller, independent services that each perform a specific function (e.g., user authentication, payment processing, or order management). These services communicate over well-defined APIs (typically RESTful APIs).

- o The microservices approach promotes modularity and makes it easier to scale individual components independently. Each service can be developed, deployed, and maintained separately, allowing for faster iteration and flexibility in choosing different technologies for different services.

When to Use Microservices Architecture:

- o **Scalable and High-Traffic Applications**: Microservices are ideal for applications that need to scale rapidly or handle high traffic loads, such as e-commerce platforms, financial systems, or social media platforms.

- o **Frequent Updates and Changes**: If your application is expected to evolve with frequent changes and feature updates, microservices make it easier to modify individual services without disrupting the entire system.

- o **Distributed Teams**: If your development team is large and spread out, microservices allow for parallel development of different services by different teams, reducing bottlenecks.

Monolithic vs. Microservices Architectures

Here, we compare the key characteristics of monolithic and microservices architectures to help you decide which one is best suited for your cross-platform enterprise application.

Feature	Monolithic Architecture	Microservices Architecture
Complexity	Easier to develop initially, but becomes complex as the application grows	More complex to develop, but easier to scale and maintain over time
Scalability	Difficult to scale, as all components are tightly coupled	Easy to scale individual services based on demand

41

Feature	Monolithic Architecture	Microservices Architecture
Deployment	Requires redeploying the entire application for updates	Each service can be deployed independently, enabling continuous deployment
Development Speed	Faster in early stages, as all components are integrated	Slower at first, as each service must be developed separately
Fault Tolerance	A failure in one component can impact the entire application	Failures in one service do not necessarily affect others, ensuring higher availability
Technology Flexibility	Limited; all components must use the same technology stack	Allows different services to use different technologies based on requirements
Team Collaboration	Fewer teams needed, as everything is in one codebase	Requires cross-functional teams with specialized skill sets for each service

While monolithic architectures might be suitable for small projects or MVPs (Minimum Viable Products), microservices are generally more suitable for larger, complex systems that need to scale, evolve, and maintain high availability.

Designing Scalable, Maintainable Solutions

Whether you choose a monolithic or microservices architecture, your focus should be on creating scalable and maintainable solutions. Below are key principles and best practices for designing such solutions:

1. **Modularity**:
   - Break down your application into modular components that can evolve independently. This allows teams to focus on individual parts of the system and improves long-term maintainability.
   - For monolithic systems, this can be achieved through clear boundaries within the codebase, even if it's still a single system.
   - For microservices, each service should be small and focused on a single responsibility, making it easier to update and scale independently.
2. **API-First Design**:

o Design APIs before implementing features, ensuring that services (whether part of a monolith or microservices) can communicate effectively with each other. This is especially critical in microservices architecture, where different services rely heavily on APIs to communicate.

o Use RESTful APIs or gRPC (a more efficient option) for communication between services.

3. **Automated Testing and Continuous Integration**:

o Automate testing for each module or service to ensure that the application is functional and bug-free.

o Implement continuous integration (CI) tools to run tests every time code is committed. This helps maintain high code quality and allows for early detection of issues.

o In microservices, it is important to test each service independently, as well as the communication between them.

4. **Scalable Databases**:

o Use databases that can scale with your application. In a monolithic system, a single database might suffice, but in a microservices system, each service may require its own database (polyglot persistence). Use solutions like sharded databases, NoSQL databases, or distributed databases to ensure scalability.

5. **Load Balancing and Caching**:

   o Use load balancing techniques to distribute traffic efficiently across multiple instances of your application or services. This is essential in ensuring your application can handle increased traffic without performance degradation.

   o Implement caching strategies (e.g., Redis, Memcached) to reduce database load and speed up response times, particularly for data that is frequently accessed but doesn't change often.

6. **Fault Tolerance and Resilience**:

   o Design your application or services to be fault-tolerant. This means that even if one component fails, the rest of the system should continue to function normally.

   o Use patterns like circuit breakers, retries, and timeouts to handle failures in a way that doesn't disrupt the entire system.

7. **Monitoring and Logging**:

   o Set up proper monitoring tools (e.g., Prometheus, Grafana) to track the performance and health of your system. Monitoring ensures that you can detect issues in real-time and resolve them quickly.

o Use centralized logging systems (e.g., ELK stack, Splunk) to capture and aggregate logs from different services, making it easier to troubleshoot and diagnose problems.

8. **Security**:

o Implement security best practices, such as using HTTPS, encrypting sensitive data, and implementing access control to prevent unauthorized access.

o In microservices, each service should be independently secured with authentication and authorization mechanisms, such as OAuth or JWT tokens.

9. **Continuous Deployment**:

o For microservices, implement continuous deployment (CD) pipelines to automatically deploy new versions of services with minimal downtime. This ensures that updates are rolled out quickly and consistently.

10. **Cloud Infrastructure**:

- Leverage cloud platforms (e.g., AWS, Azure, Google Cloud) to host and scale your application or services. Cloud providers offer managed services for databases, load balancers, caching, and more, which can simplify scaling and maintenance.

In this chapter, we've explored the architectural decisions that influence cross-platform enterprise applications. Whether you choose a monolithic or microservices architecture, the key is to focus on building scalable, maintainable solutions that can grow and evolve with the business. By following best practices in modularity, testing, fault tolerance, and security, you can design a system that meets the demands of modern enterprises and provides a solid foundation for future growth.

CHAPTER 5

UNDERSTANDING .NET CORE AND PYTHON ECOSYSTEMS

In this chapter, we will explore the ecosystems of .NET Core and Python and how these technologies are leveraged for enterprise-grade applications. We'll cover an overview of .NET Core's role in cross-platform enterprise development, highlight key Python libraries and frameworks that support cross-platform development, and discuss how to integrate these ecosystems seamlessly to build robust, scalable applications.

Overview of .NET Core for Enterprise Applications

What is .NET Core? .NET Core is an open-source, cross-platform framework developed by Microsoft, designed to build high-performance, scalable applications. It allows developers to create applications that run on Windows, macOS, and Linux. .NET Core is the foundation for developing applications that can be easily deployed to a wide variety of environments, from desktops to cloud-based infrastructure.

Key Features of .NET Core:

1. **Cross-Platform Compatibility**:
   o .NET Core was built with cross-platform compatibility in mind. Unlike the earlier versions of .NET, which were limited to Windows, .NET Core supports Linux and macOS, making it ideal for developers building applications for multiple platforms.

2. **High Performance**:
   o .NET Core is optimized for speed, with features like just-in-time (JIT) compilation, which helps improve the performance of applications, particularly in enterprise environments where efficiency is crucial.

3. **Modular and Lightweight**:
   o .NET Core is modular, meaning developers can choose and install only the parts of the framework they need. This reduces the application's footprint and improves performance.

4. **Unified Framework**:
   o .NET Core unifies the .NET ecosystem, allowing developers to use the same framework for building web apps, desktop apps, microservices, APIs, and more. It provides everything from a

simple HTTP server to an advanced cloud-native solution.

5. **Rich Ecosystem**:
   o With access to a vast set of libraries and tools, .NET Core provides a full-stack development experience. It includes libraries for web development (ASP.NET Core), database access (Entity Framework Core), and even cloud integration (Azure SDKs).

6. **Containerization and Cloud-Native Support**:
   o .NET Core supports Docker containers and is ideal for building cloud-native applications. The framework integrates seamlessly with popular cloud platforms, particularly Microsoft Azure, allowing enterprises to deploy scalable applications in a cloud environment.

7. **Security**:
   o Built with security in mind, .NET Core supports modern security protocols like OAuth2, JWT, and data protection APIs, helping ensure that enterprise applications are secure and meet regulatory requirements.

Use Cases for .NET Core in Enterprises:

- **Web Applications**: Building high-performance, scalable web applications using ASP.NET Core.

- **Microservices**: Developing and deploying microservices in cloud environments with Docker and Kubernetes.
- **APIs**: Creating RESTful APIs that can be consumed by various client applications (mobile, desktop, web).
- **Cloud-Native Solutions**: Building enterprise solutions that integrate with cloud platforms like Microsoft Azure.

Key Python Libraries and Frameworks for Cross-Platform Development

Python, being a versatile and dynamic language, boasts an extensive ecosystem of libraries and frameworks that are used in cross-platform development. The simplicity and readability of Python code make it an ideal choice for developers working on cross-platform applications that need to run seamlessly on different operating systems.

Here are some key Python libraries and frameworks that facilitate cross-platform development:

1. **Flask**:
   - Flask is a lightweight Python web framework used to build web applications and RESTful APIs. It is minimalistic, making it easy to get started, and flexible, allowing developers to add components as needed. Flask supports cross-

platform development by being able to run on any operating system with a Python interpreter.

2. **Django**:

   o Django is a high-level web framework that encourages rapid development and clean, pragmatic design. It's often used to build more feature-rich applications, such as content management systems, e-commerce sites, and large-scale enterprise applications. Like Flask, Django is cross-platform and works well on all major operating systems.

3. **PyQt**:

   o PyQt is a set of Python bindings for the Qt application framework. It's used to develop graphical user interfaces (GUIs) that can run across platforms (Windows, macOS, and Linux). It allows Python developers to build desktop applications with a native look and feel, regardless of the operating system.

4. **Kivy**:

   o Kivy is a popular open-source Python library for developing multi-touch applications. It supports Windows, macOS, Linux, Android, and iOS, making it an excellent choice for building cross-platform mobile apps as well as desktop applications.

5. **PyInstaller**:
   - PyInstaller is a tool used to package Python applications into standalone executables. It makes Python applications easy to distribute and deploy across different operating systems. PyInstaller allows you to bundle all dependencies, so the application runs without needing a Python interpreter installed on the target machine.

6. **SQLAlchemy**:
   - SQLAlchemy is an ORM (Object Relational Mapper) that provides a set of high-level APIs for connecting to relational databases. It abstracts away database-specific details, making it easy to develop cross-platform database-backed applications in Python.

7. **Celery**:
   - Celery is a distributed task queue that is often used in enterprise applications to handle asynchronous workloads. It can be configured to run on different platforms, allowing developers to scale their applications efficiently across multiple machines.

8. **Tornado**:
   - Tornado is a Python web framework and asynchronous networking library that is designed

to handle large numbers of simultaneous connections. It's often used in real-time applications, such as chat servers or live dashboards, and it works across platforms with minimal configuration.

Integration of .NET Core and Python Ecosystems in a Seamless Manner

While both .NET Core and Python are powerful in their own right, integrating them to work together in a cross-platform environment can unlock even greater potential, particularly in enterprise applications. Here's how you can seamlessly integrate these two ecosystems:

1. **Using APIs for Communication**:
   o One of the most effective ways to integrate Python and C# in a cross-platform application is through API-based communication. You can expose RESTful APIs using ASP.NET Core (C#) and consume these APIs in a Python application (or vice versa). By making both Python and C# components interact through APIs, you can leverage the strengths of both ecosystems.
   o For example, a Python-based machine learning model can be deployed as a REST API using Flask or Django, while the main enterprise

application (developed in .NET Core) communicates with it to perform tasks like data analysis or predictions.

2. **Messaging Queues**:

    o For more complex workflows, you can use message queues such as RabbitMQ or Apache Kafka to facilitate communication between Python and C# services. In this scenario, Python and C# applications send messages (e.g., job requests or results) to a message broker, and the broker ensures that the messages are delivered to the appropriate services. This approach is highly scalable and works well for microservices architectures.

3. **Shared Databases**:

    o Both .NET Core and Python can interact with the same database, making it easier to share data across systems. Using an ORM like SQLAlchemy in Python and Entity Framework Core in .NET, both languages can communicate with a common database and retrieve or update data as needed. For larger applications, a distributed database system might be used to handle scalability and fault tolerance.

4. **Using Docker**:

o Docker containers can be used to run both .NET Core and Python applications in isolated environments. By containerizing each component, you can ensure that they run consistently across different platforms. Docker also simplifies deployment, as both Python and C# applications can be packaged in their own containers and run together in a unified environment.

5. **Shared Services via Cloud**:

o For cloud-based enterprise applications, integrating .NET Core and Python services can be done using cloud-native technologies. For example, both C# and Python applications can be deployed on Microsoft Azure, where they can communicate through cloud-based messaging, APIs, or cloud databases.

In this chapter, we've explored the strengths of both the .NET Core and Python ecosystems and how they can be used for building enterprise-level cross-platform applications. By integrating these ecosystems via APIs, message queues, shared databases, and cloud services, businesses can leverage the strengths of both languages to create powerful and scalable applications that run seamlessly across platforms.

CHAPTER 6

DATA HANDLING AND INTEGRATION STRATEGIES

Data handling and integration are crucial aspects of any cross-platform application, particularly when dealing with enterprise-grade solutions that require reliable, efficient access to databases. In this chapter, we will explore how to manage and integrate data in cross-platform apps, discuss the role of Object-Relational Mappers (ORMs) like Entity Framework and SQLAlchemy, and provide real-world examples of database integration in cross-platform environments.

Working with Databases in Cross-Platform Apps

When developing cross-platform applications, the database layer plays a critical role in ensuring that data is accessible, consistent, and secure across multiple platforms. The database can be local (on the user's machine) or remote (in a cloud-based or enterprise environment), depending on the application's requirements.

Key Considerations for Database Integration:

1. **Platform Compatibility**:
   - The database solution must support the platforms on which the application will run. For example, SQLite can be used for local storage in mobile and desktop applications, while cloud databases like MySQL, PostgreSQL, or Microsoft SQL Server are ideal for enterprise-level solutions.
   - If your app needs to interact with different types of databases across platforms (e.g., PostgreSQL on Linux and SQL Server on Windows), ensure that the database technology is compatible with all the environments your application supports.

2. **Database Connectivity**:
   - For cloud-based databases, the application can connect through APIs or direct database connections. Many cloud databases provide SDKs or connection libraries for Python and .NET Core, making integration seamless.
   - Cross-platform applications may need to handle various network configurations (such as firewalls, proxy servers, or VPNs) to ensure secure and reliable database access, particularly in distributed environments.

3. **Data Sync and Offline Support**:

o In mobile and desktop cross-platform apps, data synchronization and offline support are crucial. Technologies like SQLite (for local data storage) or hybrid solutions like Realm or Firebase allow data to be cached locally and then synced with a remote database when the device is online.

Using ORMs (Object-Relational Mappers)

ORMs are essential tools in modern database management. They allow developers to interact with databases using object-oriented programming principles, eliminating the need to write raw SQL queries. ORMs are especially valuable in cross-platform development as they help abstract away the differences between database systems, providing a uniform interface regardless of the underlying platform.

Entity Framework (EF) Core for C#:

Entity Framework (EF) Core is a lightweight, cross-platform ORM for .NET Core. It allows developers to interact with a variety of databases using C# objects instead of writing SQL queries directly. EF Core supports a wide range of relational databases like SQL Server, PostgreSQL, MySQL, and SQLite, making it suitable for cross-platform applications.

Key Features of Entity Framework Core:

1. **Cross-Platform Support:**
   - ○ EF Core supports multiple database backends, including SQL Server, SQLite, PostgreSQL, and MySQL, and works seamlessly across Windows, macOS, and Linux.

2. **Code-First Approach:**
   - ○ EF Core allows developers to define the database schema using C# classes, which are then mapped to database tables. This approach promotes maintainability and allows for database changes to be managed within the codebase.

3. **LINQ Queries:**
   - ○ With EF Core, you can use Language Integrated Query (LINQ) to write database queries in C#. LINQ queries are translated into SQL by EF Core, making it easier to write complex queries in an object-oriented manner.

4. **Migration Support:**
   - ○ EF Core provides migration tools that allow developers to manage changes to the database schema over time. This is particularly useful in enterprise environments where the database schema evolves as the application grows.

SQLAlchemy for Python:

SQLAlchemy is a widely-used ORM for Python that supports multiple relational database systems, including SQLite, MySQL, PostgreSQL, and Oracle. Like Entity Framework, SQLAlchemy abstracts the database layer and allows developers to interact with the database using Python objects.

Key Features of SQLAlchemy:

1. **Cross-Platform Compatibility**:
   o SQLAlchemy works on all major platforms, including Windows, macOS, and Linux, making it ideal for cross-platform Python applications. It supports several database systems like MySQL, PostgreSQL, SQLite, and Oracle.

2. **Declarative ORM**:
   o SQLAlchemy provides a declarative system where you can define your database schema as Python classes. This enables you to interact with the database using Python objects, avoiding direct SQL queries for common tasks.

3. **SQL Expression Language**:
   o For more complex queries, SQLAlchemy provides a powerful SQL Expression Language,

allowing developers to build raw SQL queries programmatically, ensuring full flexibility when needed.

4. **Session Management**:

   o SQLAlchemy's session management system allows developers to handle transactions efficiently and provides easy access to data. It's especially useful in scenarios where the application needs to interact with the database in an isolated and consistent way.

Real-World Examples of Database Integration

1. **E-commerce Application (C# with Entity Framework Core)**: A large e-commerce company needed a cross-platform application that could run on both web and mobile devices. The application was built using .NET Core, with Entity Framework Core as the ORM for managing product inventory, customer data, and order histories.

   o **Solution**: The company used EF Core to map their C# models to a SQL Server database. With EF Core's migration tools, they were able to manage schema changes over time and deploy them to production with minimal downtime.

63

o **Benefits**: EF Core's cross-platform support allowed the application to run on both Windows (for internal servers) and Linux (for cloud-based deployment). The team used LINQ to build complex queries for filtering products, processing customer orders, and managing inventory, significantly speeding up development and ensuring maintainability.

2. **Data Analytics Dashboard (Python with SQLAlchemy)**: A data analytics firm built a cross-platform dashboard using Python to visualize key business metrics. The dashboard pulled data from a PostgreSQL database and provided real-time updates on various metrics like sales, website traffic, and customer behavior.

   o **Solution**: The firm used SQLAlchemy to interact with the PostgreSQL database, using Python objects to represent various metrics and data tables. The application supported both web and desktop interfaces using Flask (for web) and PyQt (for desktop).

   o **Benefits**: SQLAlchemy's flexibility allowed the firm to write complex queries and perform aggregations directly in Python, making the codebase easier to manage. The use of SQLAlchemy's session management ensured that data transactions were handled efficiently, even when the app had to process large datasets.

3. **Mobile Health Application (C# with SQLite)**: A healthcare startup developed a mobile application for tracking patient health metrics. The app needed to function offline and sync data with a remote server when an internet connection was available. SQLite was used for local data storage, and the app was developed using .NET Core for cross-platform compatibility between Android and iOS.

   o **Solution**: The app used SQLite to store health data locally on the device, ensuring that users could continue logging information even without an internet connection. When the device was online, the app synced the data with a cloud-based database hosted on Azure.

   o **Benefits**: Using SQLite as a local database ensured that the app could function offline, while .NET Core's cross-platform support allowed the app to be deployed on both Android and iOS. The app's performance was optimized for mobile devices by using Entity Framework Core for efficient local database queries.

4. **Financial Services Platform (Python with SQLAlchemy and Flask)**: A financial services

platform was developed to handle transactions, client accounts, and risk management for global clients. The backend was built using Flask (for RESTful API services) and SQLAlchemy (for database interaction). The platform needed to be highly secure and capable of handling real-time transactions.

- o **Solution**: SQLAlchemy was used for managing the relational database backend, with Flask serving as the API layer that allowed different front-end applications (web and mobile) to access the data. The application integrated with third-party payment systems, and SQLAlchemy handled the transaction logic.

- o **Benefits**: SQLAlchemy's ORM capabilities allowed developers to easily manage client data, transaction logs, and financial records while maintaining data consistency. The ability to write raw SQL queries using SQLAlchemy's Expression Language helped the team handle complex transaction scenarios.

In this chapter, we've covered the importance of data handling and integration in cross-platform applications. By using ORMs like Entity Framework Core for C# and

SQLAlchemy for Python, developers can abstract database complexities, streamline development, and ensure seamless integration with cross-platform systems. The real-world examples provided demonstrate how these tools can be used to build robust, scalable, and maintainable enterprise applications that work efficiently across multiple platforms.

CHAPTER 7

RESTFUL APIS: BUILDING AND CONSUMING ACROSS PLATFORMS

RESTful APIs (Representational State Transfer APIs) have become the standard for building web services due to their simplicity, scalability, and ease of integration across different platforms. In this chapter, we will dive into the fundamentals of RESTful API design, explain how to build APIs using C# and Python, and explore how to consume and integrate APIs between C# and Python applications for cross-platform communication.

The Fundamentals of RESTful API Design

REST is an architectural style for designing networked applications. It relies on a stateless, client-server communication model where resources are represented by URLs, and interactions with those resources are conducted using standard HTTP methods like GET, POST, PUT, and DELETE.

Key principles of RESTful API design include:

1. **Statelessness**:
   - Each API request is independent of the previous ones. The server does not store any state about the client between requests, making RESTful APIs scalable and easy to cache. Each request must contain all the necessary information (e.g., authentication, data) for the server to process it.

2. **Resource-Based**:
   - In RESTful APIs, resources (e.g., users, orders, products) are identified by unique URLs. The server provides access to these resources via HTTP methods:
     - **GET**: Retrieve a resource or a list of resources.
     - **POST**: Create a new resource.
     - **PUT**: Update an existing resource.
     - **DELETE**: Remove a resource.

3. **Uniform Interface**:
   - REST APIs are designed to provide a consistent and simple interface for interacting with resources. This means using predictable URLs, standard HTTP methods, and a well-defined response format (usually JSON or XML).

4. **HTTP Status Codes**:

- o RESTful APIs use standard HTTP status codes to indicate the outcome of a request:
  - **200 OK**: Request was successful.
  - **201 Created**: A new resource was successfully created.
  - **400 Bad Request**: The request was malformed or missing parameters.
  - **401 Unauthorized**: The client is not authenticated.
  - **404 Not Found**: The requested resource could not be found.
  - **500 Internal Server Error**: An error occurred on the server.

5. **HATEOAS (Hypermedia As The Engine of Application State)**:
   - o In advanced RESTful APIs, HATEOAS is used to provide clients with links to related resources in API responses. This allows clients to dynamically discover available actions or resources.

Building APIs with C# and Python

Building APIs with C# (ASP.NET Core): ASP.NET Core is a powerful framework for building RESTful APIs in C#. It is cross-platform and can run on Windows, macOS, and

Linux. With its simplicity and scalability, ASP.NET Core is widely used in enterprise-level applications.

1. **Setting Up an API with ASP.NET Core**:

   o To build an API, start by creating a new ASP.NET Core Web API project in Visual Studio.

   o Install the necessary packages for API development, such as `Microsoft.AspNetCore.Mvc` for building RESTful services.

   o Define your API controllers using the `[ApiController]` attribute and create routes for different HTTP methods.

   o Example:

```csharp
Copy
using Microsoft.AspNetCore.Mvc;

[Route("api/[controller]")]
[ApiController]
public class ProductsController : ControllerBase
{
    private static List<Product>
products = new List<Product>();
```

```
// GET: api/products
[HttpGet]
public
ActionResult<IEnumerable<Product>>
Get()
    {
        return Ok(products);
    }

// POST: api/products
[HttpPost]
public      ActionResult<Product>
Post(Product product)
    {
        products.Add(product);
        return
CreatedAtAction(nameof(Get),   new   {
id = product.Id }, product);
    }
}
```

2. **Setting Up Authentication and Authorization**:

   o   You can secure your API by adding JWT (JSON Web Token) authentication or OAuth2.0 using middleware in ASP.NET Core. This ensures that only authorized clients can access certain resources.

3. **Testing Your API**:

o ASP.NET Core provides integrated support for testing APIs through tools like Postman or Swagger, which automatically generates API documentation and testing interfaces.

Building APIs with Python (Flask): Flask is a lightweight and flexible Python web framework often used for building RESTful APIs. It allows rapid development with minimal boilerplate code.

1. **Setting Up an API with Flask**:
    o Install Flask using `pip install Flask`.
    o Create a new Python file to define your API routes and resources.
    o Example:

```python
Copy
from flask import Flask, jsonify, request

app = Flask(__name__)

products = []

@app.route('/api/products',
methods=['GET'])
def get_products():
```

73

```
        return jsonify(products)

@app.route('/api/products',
methods=['POST'])
def add_product():
    product = request.get_json()
    products.append(product)
    return jsonify(product), 201

if __name__ == '__main__':
    app.run(debug=True)
```

2. **Handling Errors**:
   o   Flask allows you to define custom error handlers
       for HTTP status codes (e.g., 400, 404, 500). This
       is crucial for ensuring that the client receives
       meaningful feedback on failed requests.

3. **Testing Your API**:
   o   Similar to ASP.NET Core, Flask APIs can be
       tested using tools like Postman or curl. Flask also
       has built-in support for unit testing with
       `unittest` or `pytest`.

Consuming and Integrating APIs Between C# and Python Apps

Once you have built your APIs, you will likely need to
consume them in other parts of your application, such as a
client app or another microservice. Let's explore how to

consume and integrate APIs between C# and Python applications.

Consuming APIs in C#:

1. **Using HttpClient to Call REST APIs**:
   - In C#, the `HttpClient` class is used to send HTTP requests to APIs and retrieve responses.
   - Example of calling a REST API:

```csharp
Copy
using System;
using System.Net.Http;
using System.Threading.Tasks;

public class ApiClient
{
    private static readonly HttpClient client = new HttpClient();

    public async Task GetProductsAsync()
    {
        var response = await client.GetStringAsync("http://localhost:5000/api/products");
```

```csharp
Console.WriteLine(response);
    }


    public        async        Task
AddProductAsync(Product product)
    {
        var   content   =   new
StringContent(

JsonConvert.SerializeObject(product
),
            Encoding.UTF8,
            "application/json"
        );
        var   response   =   await
client.PostAsync("http://localhost:
5000/api/products", content);

Console.WriteLine(response.StatusCo
de);
    }
}
```

2. **Handling API Responses**:

o   After making an API call, you can deserialize the response using libraries like `Json.NET` to convert the JSON response into C# objects.

Consuming APIs in Python:

1. **Using the `requests` Library**:
   - The `requests` library in Python is commonly used to make HTTP requests to RESTful APIs. It's simple and powerful, with built-in methods for handling various HTTP methods like GET, POST, PUT, and DELETE.
   - Example of calling a REST API in Python:

   ```python
   Copy
   import requests
   import json

   def get_products():
       response                    =
   requests.get('http://localhost:5000
   /api/products')
       print(response.json())

   def add_product(product):
       response = requests.post(

   'http://localhost:5000/api/products
   ',
           json=product
       )
       print(response.status_code)
   ```

77

2. **Error Handling**:

   o Use `try-except` blocks to handle potential issues when making API calls, such as connection errors, timeouts, or non-200 HTTP status codes.

Integrating C# and Python APIs: If your C# application needs to consume Python-based APIs or vice versa, both systems can communicate via HTTP requests. The C# application can make `HttpClient` requests to a Python-based Flask API, and the Python application can use the `requests` library to call APIs hosted by a C#-based ASP.NET Core application.

Example Use Case: E-Commerce Platform:

- Imagine an e-commerce platform where the backend is built in C# using ASP.NET Core, and certain product recommendation features are handled by a Python-based machine learning API.
- The C# API might expose product data and receive user interactions, while the Python API takes the user interaction data (e.g., browsing history, clicks) and returns product recommendations.
- This integration allows the frontend or mobile app (whether in Python or C#) to communicate seamlessly with both systems.

In this chapter, we've explored the fundamentals of RESTful API design, the process of building APIs with C# and Python, and how to consume and integrate APIs between these two ecosystems. By using standard HTTP methods and best practices, developers can create flexible and scalable APIs that allow different platforms and technologies to communicate with each other, enabling cross-platform interoperability in enterprise-grade applications.

CHAPTER 8

SECURITY BEST PRACTICES FOR CROSS-PLATFORM SOLUTIONS

Security is a critical aspect of any software development process, especially for cross-platform applications that handle sensitive data and interact with various external services. In this chapter, we will explore secure coding practices for Python and C#, authentication and authorization strategies, including OAuth and JWT, and methods for handling sensitive data and encryption in cross-platform solutions.

Secure Coding Practices for Python and C#

Secure coding practices are essential for protecting applications from common vulnerabilities, such as SQL injection, cross-site scripting (XSS), and buffer overflow attacks. Below are best practices for secure coding in both Python and C#.

Python Secure Coding Practices:

1. **Input Validation**:

- o Always validate and sanitize user inputs to avoid common vulnerabilities like SQL injection or XSS. Use parameterized queries for database access to prevent SQL injection.
- o **Example** (Using parameterized queries with sqlite3):

```python
Copy
import sqlite3

def fetch_user_data(user_id):
    conn = sqlite3.connect('database.db')
    cursor = conn.cursor()
    cursor.execute("SELECT * FROM users WHERE user_id = ?", (user_id,))
    return cursor.fetchone()
```

2. **Avoid Hardcoding Sensitive Information**:

- o Never hardcode sensitive information such as passwords, API keys, or database connection strings in your codebase. Use environment variables or configuration files with proper access controls.
- o **Example**:

```python
python
```

```
Copy
import os

db_password                    =
os.getenv('DB_PASSWORD')
```

3. **Use Secure Dependencies**:
   - Regularly update your dependencies to fix security vulnerabilities in third-party libraries. Use tools like `pip-audit` or `safety` to identify insecure packages in your environment.

4. **Cross-Site Scripting (XSS) Prevention**:
   - For web applications, sanitize user input before rendering it in HTML, ensuring that user-generated content cannot inject malicious scripts into your app. Libraries like `Flask-Security` or `Bleach` can help sanitize input.
   - **Example**:

```python
Copy
from bleach import clean

safe_input = clean(user_input)
```

C# Secure Coding Practices:

1. **Use Parameterized Queries**:

- o Like Python, C# developers should use parameterized queries when interacting with databases to prevent SQL injection attacks.
- o **Example** (Using Entity Framework):

```csharp
Copy
using (var context = new MyDbContext())
{
    var user = context.Users.Where(u => u.UserId == userId).FirstOrDefault();
}
```

2. **Input Validation**:

- o Ensure that all user inputs are validated against expected types and ranges. Use built-in validation attributes like [Required], [Range], and [EmailAddress] to enforce validation.
- o **Example**:

```csharp
Copy
public class User
{
    [Required]
    [StringLength(100)]
    public string Name { get; set; }
```

```
}
```

3. **Use Strong Hashing for Passwords**:
   - Never store plain-text passwords. Use strong hashing algorithms like bcrypt or PBKDF2 to hash passwords before storing them in the database. The .NET framework offers the `PasswordHasher<T>` class for password hashing.
   - **Example**:

   ```csharp
   Copy
   var passwordHasher = new
   PasswordHasher<User>();
   var hashedPassword =
   passwordHasher.HashPassword(user,
   password);
   ```

4. **Secure Communication (TLS/SSL)**:
   - Always ensure that sensitive data is transmitted securely over HTTPS by enforcing the use of TLS (Transport Layer Security) in web applications.
   - **Example** (ASP.NET Core configuration):

   ```csharp
   Copy
   ```

```
app.UseHttpsRedirection();
```

Authentication and Authorization Strategies (OAuth, JWT)

In any cross-platform solution, securing user authentication and authorizing access to resources is essential. The most commonly used authentication mechanisms are OAuth and JWT (JSON Web Tokens).

OAuth:

OAuth is an open standard for authorization that allows third-party applications to access resources on behalf of a user, without sharing the user's credentials. OAuth 2.0 is the most widely used version for modern web and mobile applications.

1. **OAuth 2.0 Flow**:
    o The typical OAuth 2.0 flow involves the following steps:
        1. The user is redirected to an OAuth provider (e.g., Google, Facebook).
        2. The user grants permission for the application to access certain resources.
        3. The OAuth provider returns an access token to the application.

4. The application uses the access token to make authorized API requests on behalf of the user.

2. **Implementing OAuth in C#:**

   o **ASP.NET Core** has built-in support for OAuth 2.0, making it easy to integrate OAuth-based authentication with external providers.

   o Example (Using Google OAuth in ASP.NET Core):

```csharp
Copy
public                          void
ConfigureServices(IServiceCollectio
n services)
{

services.AddAuthentication(options
=>
    {
        options.DefaultScheme     =
CookieAuthenticationDefaults.Authen
ticationScheme;

options.DefaultChallengeScheme     =
GoogleDefaults.AuthenticationScheme
;
    })
    .AddCookie()
```

86

```
.AddGoogle(options =>
{
    options.ClientId       =
Configuration["Google:ClientId"];
    options.ClientSecret   =
Configuration["Google:ClientSecret"
];
});
}
```

3. **OAuth in Python**:

   o Python developers can use the `requests-oauthlib` library to integrate OAuth authentication into their applications.

   o Example (Using OAuth 2.0 with `requests` in Python):

```python
Copy
from requests_oauthlib import
OAuth2Session

oauth                      =
OAuth2Session(client_id='your-
client-id',        redirect_uri='your-
redirect-uri')
authorization_url,      state    =
oauth.authorization_url('https://pr
ovider.com/oauth/authorize')
```

JWT (JSON Web Tokens):

JWT is a compact, URL-safe token format used for securely transmitting information between parties. It is commonly used for stateless authentication in web and mobile applications.

1. **JWT Structure**:
   - A JWT consists of three parts:
      1. **Header**: Contains the token type (JWT) and signing algorithm.
      2. **Payload**: Contains the claims (user information, roles, etc.).
      3. **Signature**: Ensures the integrity of the token.

2. **JWT Authentication in C#**:
   - You can use the `System.IdentityModel.Tokens.Jwt` package in C# to issue and validate JWTs.
   - Example (Generating JWT in ASP.NET Core):

```csharp
Copy
var securityKey = new
SymmetricSecurityKey(Encoding.UTF8.
GetBytes("your_secret_key"));
```

```
var        credentials    =        new
SigningCredentials(securityKey,
SecurityAlgorithms.HmacSha256);
var token = new JwtSecurityToken(
    issuer: "your-issuer",
    audience: "your-audience",
    expires:
DateTime.Now.AddMinutes(30),
    signingCredentials: credentials
);
var        tokenHandler    =        new
JwtSecurityTokenHandler();
string              jwtToken            =
tokenHandler.WriteToken(token);
```

3. JWT Authentication in Python:

- o The PyJWT library is commonly used in Python for creating and verifying JWT tokens.
- o Example (Generating JWT in Python):

```python
Copy
import jwt
import datetime

payload = {
    'user_id': 123,
```

```
             'exp':
datetime.datetime.utcnow()              +
datetime.timedelta(minutes=30)
}
secret_key = 'your_secret_key'
token      =      jwt.encode(payload,
secret_key, algorithm='HS256')
```

Handling Sensitive Data and Encryption

Encryption is a critical component of securing sensitive data in any application, particularly when dealing with personal information, payment details, or any other confidential data.

1. **Data Encryption at Rest**:
   - o Sensitive data stored in databases, files, or cloud storage should be encrypted to protect it from unauthorized access. Use strong encryption algorithms such as AES (Advanced Encryption Standard) to encrypt data at rest.
   - o In both Python and C#, encryption libraries like `Cryptography` (Python) and `System.Security.Cryptography` (C#) can be used for this purpose.
   - o **Example (AES encryption in C#)**:

   ```csharp
   csharp
   ```

```
Copy
using (Aes aesAlg = Aes.Create())
{
    aesAlg.Key                    =
Encoding.UTF8.GetBytes("your-16-
byte-key");
    aesAlg.IV                     =
Encoding.UTF8.GetBytes("your-16-
byte-IV");
    ICryptoTransform  encryptor   =
aesAlg.CreateEncryptor(aesAlg.Key,
aesAlg.IV);
    // Use encryptor to encrypt data
}
```

2. **Data Encryption in Transit**:

   o Always use HTTPS (SSL/TLS) to encrypt data during transmission between clients and servers. This ensures that sensitive data such as passwords, payment details, and personal information are protected from man-in-the-middle (MITM) attacks.

3. **Key Management**:

   o Store encryption keys securely using key management systems (e.g., AWS KMS, Azure Key Vault, or HashiCorp Vault). Never hardcode encryption keys in your codebase.

In this chapter, we've covered critical security best practices for building cross-platform applications. We explored secure coding practices for Python and C#, authentication strategies like OAuth and JWT, and methods for handling sensitive data and encryption. By following these security best practices, you can protect your applications from common vulnerabilities and ensure that your cross-platform solutions remain safe, secure, and reliable.

CHAPTER 9

PERFORMANCE OPTIMIZATION ACROSS PLATFORMS

Performance is one of the most important aspects of building cross-platform applications, especially when they need to run efficiently across different operating systems and devices. In this chapter, we will explore performance profiling tools for both Python and C#, best practices for optimizing application performance, and real-world examples of performance improvements to demonstrate how these practices are applied.

Performance Profiling Tools for Python and C#

To optimize the performance of your cross-platform applications, it's crucial to first understand where the performance bottlenecks lie. Profiling tools are essential for measuring and identifying areas of your application that consume excessive CPU, memory, or other resources. Let's take a look at some common profiling tools available for both Python and C#.

Python Performance Profiling Tools:

1. **cProfile**:
   - **cProfile** is the built-in Python profiler, which provides a detailed analysis of the functions in your program. It can be used to measure how many times each function is called and how much time is spent in each function.
   - **Usage**:

```python
Copy
import cProfile

def my_function():
    # Your function code
    pass

cProfile.run('my_function()')
```

   - **Output**: It shows the number of calls to each function and the total time spent in each one, allowing you to identify which parts of your code need optimization.
2. **line_profiler**:
   - The **line_profiler** tool provides a more granular level of profiling by measuring time at the

94

individual line level. This can be particularly useful when you need to pinpoint slow lines of code.

- o **Installation**: Install with `pip install line_profiler`.
- o **Usage**: Use the `@profile` decorator to mark the functions you want to profile.

```python
Copy
@profile
def my_function():
    # Your function code
    pass
```

3. **memory_profiler**:

- o **memory_profiler** is useful for profiling memory usage in Python applications. It helps you track the memory consumption of your functions and identify memory leaks.
- o **Installation**: Install with `pip install memory_profiler`.
- o **Usage**:

```python
Copy
from memory_profiler import profile
```

```
@profile
def my_function():
    # Your function code
    pass
```

4. **Py-Spy**:

   o **Py-Spy** is an external Python profiler that works without requiring modifications to your code. It can be used to monitor a running Python application and profile its performance in real-time.

   o **Installation**: Install with `pip install py-spy`.

   o **Usage**: Run `py-spy top` to see a live snapshot of where your Python application is spending its time.

C# Performance Profiling Tools:

1. **Visual Studio Profiler**:

   o Visual Studio provides a built-in profiler that allows developers to track CPU usage, memory usage, and the performance of different code segments in their C# applications.

   o **Usage**: In Visual Studio, you can start profiling by going to **Debug** > **Performance Profiler**. This

96

will provide real-time metrics on CPU usage, memory allocation, and more.

2. **BenchmarkDotNet**:

   o **BenchmarkDotNet** is a popular library in C# for performance benchmarking. It provides highly accurate performance measurement tools and is used to benchmark individual methods or code segments.

   o **Installation**: Install with NuGet: `Install-Package BenchmarkDotNet`.

   o **Usage**:

```csharp
Copy
using BenchmarkDotNet.Attributes;
using BenchmarkDotNet.Running;

public class MyBenchmark
{
    [Benchmark]
    public void MyMethod()
    {
        // Method code
    }

    public static void Main(string[] args)
    {
```

```
        var        summary        =
BenchmarkRunner.Run<MyBenchmark>();
    }
}
```

3. **dotTrace**:

   o **dotTrace** is a performance profiler from JetBrains, designed to analyze C# code for memory and CPU usage. It helps you identify performance bottlenecks, deadlocks, and memory leaks.

   o **Usage**: Install dotTrace and run it alongside your C# application to get detailed reports on memory consumption and CPU usage.

4. **PerfView**:

   o **PerfView** is a performance analysis tool from Microsoft. It helps developers collect and analyze data about the CPU, memory, and other performance metrics in .NET applications.

   o **Usage**: Launch PerfView and start collecting data. Afterward, you can analyze stack traces and time spent in different parts of the application.

Best Practices for Optimizing Application Performance

After identifying performance bottlenecks using profiling tools, it's important to apply best practices for optimization.

Below are several strategies to improve the performance of your cross-platform application.

1. **Optimize Algorithms**:
   - Always ensure that your algorithms have the best time and space complexity for the problem at hand. Avoid inefficient operations like unnecessary nested loops or excessive data copying. Instead, focus on optimizing core algorithms that are critical for the performance of the application.

2. **Efficient Memory Usage**:
   - In both Python and C#, try to minimize memory usage by efficiently managing data structures. Avoid memory leaks by ensuring that objects that are no longer needed are released.
   - Use memory-efficient data structures like `deque` in Python or `List<T>` in C# instead of arrays where applicable.
   - Use memory pools in both languages for managing large amounts of memory.

3. **Lazy Loading and Caching**:
   - Lazy loading allows you to load data only when it's needed, rather than loading everything at once, which can lead to performance degradation.

o Implement caching strategies to store frequently used data temporarily, reducing database or API calls and improving response times. For example, use `Redis` for caching in C# or Python applications.

4. **Parallelism and Asynchronous Programming**:

o In applications that require heavy computation or data processing, use parallelism and asynchronous programming to split tasks across multiple threads or processors.

o **Python**: Use the `asyncio` library or multi-threading/multi-processing for parallel tasks.

o **C#**: Use the `Task` class and `async/await` keywords for asynchronous operations. You can also take advantage of parallel programming with `Parallel.For` and `Parallel.ForEach`.

5. **Minimize I/O Operations**:

o Excessive I/O operations (file reads/writes, network requests, etc.) can slow down an application. Use asynchronous I/O wherever possible and batch I/O operations to minimize delays.

o Use compression when transmitting large files or data over the network to reduce transmission times.

6. **Optimize Database Queries**:

100

- o Optimize database queries by ensuring that indexes are used efficiently and avoiding N+1 query problems.
- o In Python, use `SQLAlchemy` or `Django ORM` to ensure efficient querying and minimize unnecessary database hits. In C#, Entity Framework Core has built-in features for optimizing queries.

7. **Profile and Optimize Startup Time**:
   - o For cross-platform desktop and mobile applications, reduce startup time by lazy loading resources or pre-compiling parts of the application that do not require initialization on startup.

Real-World Examples of Performance Improvements

1. **E-Commerce Website (Python and C# Integration)**: A large e-commerce website built with Python for backend services and C# for frontend processing was experiencing performance issues with slow response times during peak shopping hours. Profiling revealed that the bottleneck was in the API calls between Python and C# services, as well as inefficient database queries.

- o **Solution**: The backend Python application was optimized by reducing the number of API calls between services and optimizing database queries with better indexing. In the C# frontend, caching was implemented for frequently accessed data (like product information) to reduce load times.

- o **Result**: The application experienced a 30% reduction in response time during peak hours and a smoother overall user experience.

2. **Data Analytics Dashboard (C# with .NET Core)**: A data analytics dashboard built with C# and .NET Core was taking longer than expected to load large datasets, especially when visualizing complex graphs. Profiling showed that the performance issue was related to inefficient data processing on the server side.

- o **Solution**: The team optimized the data processing pipeline by refactoring algorithms and using multi-threading to process large datasets in parallel. Additionally, they implemented lazy loading for certain data components and utilized Redis caching for commonly queried data.

- o **Result**: The dashboard's load time decreased by 50%, significantly improving the user experience and enabling quicker decision-making.

3. **Mobile Health Application (Python with Flask)**: A mobile health application built with Python and Flask was facing performance issues when syncing large amounts of health data from the device to the server. Profiling showed that the syncing process was excessively slow due to inefficient data serialization and network communication.

   o **Solution**: The team optimized the data serialization process using faster formats like Protocol Buffers instead of JSON and implemented asynchronous data syncing. Additionally, they compressed the data before sending it over the network.

   o **Result**: The syncing process became significantly faster, with data transfer times reduced by 40%, enhancing the mobile experience for users.

In this chapter, we covered performance profiling tools for both Python and C#, best practices for optimizing application performance, and real-world examples where performance improvements were implemented successfully. By profiling your applications and following these optimization techniques, you can ensure that your cross-platform solutions perform efficiently across different environments and devices.

CHAPTER 10

CROSS-PLATFORM UI DEVELOPMENT

In cross-platform application development, the user interface (UI) plays a crucial role in ensuring a seamless user experience across multiple platforms. Developing a UI that works well on different devices and operating systems can be challenging, but with the right tools and techniques, it's entirely possible to create an elegant, responsive UI that meets the needs of your users. In this chapter, we will explore how to build cross-platform UIs using Xamarin and PyQt, discuss best practices for designing responsive UIs, and provide a real-world example of a cross-platform enterprise-grade application.

Using Xamarin and PyQt for Building User Interfaces

Xamarin (for C#):

Xamarin is a powerful framework that allows developers to create cross-platform mobile and desktop applications using C# and .NET. It enables you to write code once and deploy it on multiple platforms, including Android, iOS, and Windows.

1. **What is Xamarin?**
   - Xamarin is based on the .NET framework, making it easy for developers familiar with C# and .NET to build mobile apps. Xamarin uses native controls on each platform to ensure a native look and feel while sharing the same codebase.

2. **Building UIs with Xamarin.Forms**:
   - Xamarin.Forms is a UI toolkit that allows you to build user interfaces that work across all supported platforms (Android, iOS, Windows, and macOS) using a shared codebase. You can design your UI using XAML (Extensible Application Markup Language) or C#.
   - Xamarin provides a set of controls, such as buttons, labels, and text boxes, which automatically render using the native controls of each platform.

Example (Xamarin.Forms UI for a simple login screen):

```csharp
Copy
```

```
public class LoginPage : ContentPage
{
    public LoginPage()
    {
        var usernameEntry = new Entry
        {
            Placeholder = "Username"
        };

        var passwordEntry = new Entry
        {
            Placeholder = "Password",
            IsPassword = true
        };

        var loginButton = new Button
        {
            Text = "Login"
        };

        loginButton.Clicked += (sender,
args) =>
        {
            // Handle login logic
        };

        Content = new StackLayout
        {
```

```
                    Children = { usernameEntry,
passwordEntry, loginButton }
        };
    }
}
```

3. **Xamarin for Enterprise Applications**:

   o Xamarin allows you to integrate with enterprise-level APIs and services, such as Azure, RESTful APIs, and enterprise databases, enabling you to create robust, scalable mobile applications. Xamarin's support for MVVM (Model-View-ViewModel) architecture also promotes a clean separation of concerns, making it easier to maintain large-scale applications.

PyQt (for Python):

PyQt is a set of Python bindings for the Qt application framework, which is used to build cross-platform applications with graphical user interfaces. PyQt supports a wide range of platforms, including Windows, macOS, and Linux, and provides tools to create desktop applications with native UIs.

1. **What is PyQt?**

o PyQt provides Python bindings to the Qt framework, a powerful and widely-used C++ toolkit for creating rich desktop applications. PyQt allows developers to create native-looking applications for various platforms without having to deal with the complexities of low-level system programming.

2. **Building UIs with PyQt**:

   o PyQt includes a wide range of UI components such as buttons, labels, sliders, and text inputs. It also offers advanced features like support for custom widgets, graphics views, and animation.

   o You can design UIs using Python code or Qt Designer (a visual design tool that generates XML-based .ui files, which can be converted into Python code).

Example (PyQt UI for a simple login screen):

```python
Copy
import sys
from PyQt5.QtWidgets import QApplication,
QWidget, QVBoxLayout, QLabel, QLineEdit,
QPushButton

class LoginWindow(QWidget):
    def __init__(self):
```

109

```python
        super().__init__()

        self.setWindowTitle("Login")
        self.setGeometry(100,   100,   300,
150)

        layout = QVBoxLayout()

        self.username = QLineEdit(self)

self.username.setPlaceholderText("Usernam
e")
        layout.addWidget(self.username)

        self.password = QLineEdit(self)

self.password.setPlaceholderText("Passwor
d")

self.password.setEchoMode(QLineEdit.Passw
ord)
        layout.addWidget(self.password)

        self.login_button               =
QPushButton("Login", self)

self.login_button.clicked.connect(self.ha
ndle_login)
```

110

```
layout.addWidget(self.login_button)

    self.setLayout(layout)

def handle_login(self):
    # Handle login logic
    print(f"Logging          in          as
{self.username.text()}")

if __name__ == "__main__":
    app = QApplication(sys.argv)
    window = LoginWindow()
    window.show()
    sys.exit(app.exec_())
```

3. **PyQt for Enterprise Applications**:

   o PyQt can be used for building powerful desktop applications in Python, with robust support for complex UIs, databases, and networking. It's particularly suitable for applications that require a native desktop experience, such as enterprise applications for finance, data analysis, and project management.

Designing Responsive UIs for Various Platforms

When building cross-platform UIs, it's important to design user interfaces that adapt to different screen sizes, resolutions, and input methods (e.g., mouse, keyboard, touch). A responsive UI ensures that your application works seamlessly across desktops, tablets, and smartphones.

Key Design Principles:

1. **Layout Flexibility**:
   o Use flexible layouts that adjust to different screen sizes. Both Xamarin.Forms and PyQt provide layout managers (e.g., `StackLayout`, `GridLayout` in Xamarin, and `QVBoxLayout`, `QHBoxLayout` in PyQt) to arrange UI elements dynamically.

2. **Avoid Fixed Dimensions**:
   o Avoid using fixed sizes for UI components. Instead, rely on relative positioning and sizing. For example, use percentages or dynamic layouts to adapt to different screen dimensions.

3. **Touch and Mouse Input**:
   o Make sure that buttons, text fields, and other interactive elements are large enough for touch interactions on mobile devices, while remaining

usable with a mouse on desktop platforms. In Xamarin, you can handle different input methods using touch gestures or mouse events.

4. **Adaptive UI**:

   o Customize the UI to reflect platform conventions (e.g., a navigation drawer in Android, a tab bar in iOS). Xamarin.Forms allows you to apply platform-specific customizations using the `Device.OnPlatform()` method, and PyQt provides tools like `QStyle` for applying native platform styles.

5. **Testing Across Devices**:

   o Test your application on a variety of devices and screen sizes. Xamarin provides an emulator for testing on Android and iOS devices, while PyQt applications can be tested on different operating systems and screen sizes to ensure consistency.

Example of a Cross-Platform Enterprise-Grade App

Let's consider a real-world example of a cross-platform enterprise-grade app built using Xamarin and PyQt. We'll look at a **task management application** that integrates with cloud-based services, supports multiple platforms, and features a native-looking UI.

Features of the Task Management App:

- **Task Creation**: Users can create, edit, and delete tasks.
- **Cloud Sync**: Tasks are synced with a cloud service (e.g., Azure or Firebase) to allow access from multiple devices.
- **Responsive UI**: The UI adapts to different screen sizes and input types (touch or mouse).
- **User Authentication**: The app uses OAuth for user login and authorization.
- **Notifications**: Push notifications are sent to remind users about upcoming tasks.

Building the App:

- **Xamarin for Mobile Apps**: The mobile app is built using Xamarin.Forms, providing a unified codebase that runs on both iOS and Android. Xamarin handles task synchronization with the cloud, authentication with OAuth, and UI rendering for mobile devices.
- **PyQt for Desktop App**: The desktop app is built using PyQt, ensuring that the application looks and feels native on Windows, macOS, and Linux. The same cloud sync and authentication features are integrated, and the UI adjusts to different screen sizes.

- **Backend Service**: The backend is developed as a RESTful API in C# using ASP.NET Core. The API handles task management, user authentication, and cloud synchronization. Both the Xamarin and PyQt apps interact with the API to manage tasks and user data.

Outcome:

- **Cross-Platform Consistency**: The app works seamlessly across mobile and desktop platforms, with a consistent user experience that adapts to each platform's conventions.
- **Efficient Code Sharing**: A significant portion of the business logic, such as task creation and authentication, is shared across platforms, reducing development and maintenance costs.
- **Enterprise-Grade Integration**: The app integrates with cloud services for data storage and user authentication, providing scalability and security for enterprise-level applications.

In this chapter, we explored how to build cross-platform UIs using Xamarin and PyQt, focusing on the design and development techniques necessary to create responsive, adaptive interfaces that work seamlessly across different devices. We also provided a real-world example of a cross-platform enterprise-grade application, showcasing the power of these tools to create professional, scalable applications for businesses.

CHAPTER 11

HANDLING ASYNCHRONOUS PROGRAMMING

Asynchronous programming is a critical concept in modern software development, especially for building high-performance, responsive applications. In this chapter, we'll explore the importance of concurrency and parallelism in enterprise applications, look at asynchronous programming techniques in Python (using `asyncio`), and dive into how C# implements asynchronous programming with `async` and `await`. We will also cover real-world use cases where asynchronous design improves performance and user experience.

Importance of Concurrency and Parallelism in Enterprise Apps

Concurrency and **parallelism** are two essential concepts that help improve the performance of applications, especially those that handle multiple tasks at once.

- **Concurrency**: Refers to the ability of an application to handle multiple tasks at the same time, but not necessarily simultaneously. In a concurrent program, tasks may start, run, and complete in overlapping time periods, allowing the program to handle more than one task at a time without waiting for each to finish before moving on to the next.

- **Parallelism**: Takes concurrency a step further by executing multiple tasks simultaneously, leveraging multiple processors or cores. Parallelism allows applications to truly run tasks in parallel, resulting in faster execution for CPU-bound tasks.

In enterprise applications, particularly those with a large number of users or those that need to handle many external requests (e.g., from databases, APIs, or file systems), leveraging concurrency and parallelism is essential. These techniques enable better resource utilization, improved scalability, and a more responsive user experience.

Asynchronous programming is a natural fit for concurrency and parallelism because it allows programs to handle multiple tasks without blocking the main thread, which is crucial for applications that rely on I/O-bound operations (e.g., reading files, making API calls, or accessing databases).

Asynchronous Programming in Python (asyncio)

Python's `asyncio` library provides a framework for writing concurrent code using the `async` and `await` keywords. It allows for writing asynchronous code that looks and behaves like synchronous code, making it easier to reason about and maintain.

1. **What is asyncio?**
    - `asyncio` is a library in Python used for writing single-threaded concurrent code. It is especially useful for I/O-bound tasks, where the application spends a lot of time waiting for external resources (like a database or an HTTP request).
    - With `asyncio`, you can run multiple tasks concurrently in an event loop without blocking the main thread, which is ideal for tasks like web scraping, making HTTP requests, or managing multiple connections in a chat application.

2. **Basic Concepts**:
    - **Event Loop**: The core of `asyncio` is the event loop, which manages and schedules asynchronous tasks.
    - **async and await**: These keywords allow you to define coroutines (asynchronous functions) and

wait for the completion of tasks without blocking the main execution flow.

3. **Example of Asynchronous Programming in Python**: Here's an example that demonstrates how to use `asyncio` to make multiple HTTP requests concurrently.

```python
Copy
import asyncio
import aiohttp

async def fetch(url):
    async with aiohttp.ClientSession() as session:
        async with session.get(url) as response:
            return await response.text()

async def main():
    urls = ['https://example.com',
'https://example.org',
'https://example.net']
    tasks = [fetch(url) for url in urls]
    results = await asyncio.gather(*tasks)
    for result in results:
        print(result)

asyncio.run(main())
```

120

Explanation:

- o   `fetch()` is an asynchronous function that makes an HTTP GET request using `aiohttp`.
- o   `main()` creates a list of tasks (one for each URL) and uses `asyncio.gather()` to run them concurrently.
- o   `asyncio.run(main())` starts the event loop and runs the asynchronous tasks.

4. **Use Cases for `asyncio`:**

- o   **Web Scraping**: If you need to scrape multiple web pages simultaneously, using `asyncio` can allow you to send requests concurrently, making the process much faster.
- o   **Network Servers**: `asyncio` is ideal for building high-performance network servers (e.g., chat servers or HTTP servers) that need to handle thousands of connections at once.

Asynchronous Programming in C# (async/await)

In C#, asynchronous programming is supported natively with the `async` and `await` keywords. C# uses a similar event-driven model to Python's `asyncio`, but it integrates more deeply with the .NET framework, providing a more seamless and powerful asynchronous programming model for both I/O-bound and CPU-bound operations.

1. **What is async/await in C#?**

   o `async` and `await` in C# allow developers to write asynchronous code that is easy to understand and maintain. The `async` keyword marks a method as asynchronous, and the `await` keyword is used to pause the execution of an asynchronous method until the awaited task completes.

2. **Basic Concepts**:

   o **Task**: In C#, asynchronous methods return a `Task` object (or `Task<T>` for methods that return a result). A `Task` represents an operation that can be awaited.

   o **async and await**: Just like Python, the `async` keyword makes a method asynchronous, and `await` pauses execution until the awaited task completes.

3. **Example of Asynchronous Programming in C#**: Here's an example using `HttpClient` to make asynchronous HTTP requests.

   ```
   csharp
   Copy
   ```

```csharp
using System;
using System.Net.Http;
using System.Threading.Tasks;

class Program
{
    static async Task Main(string[] args)
    {
        string[] urls = { "https://example.com",
"https://example.org",
"https://example.net" };
        var tasks = new Task<string>[urls.Length];

        for (int i = 0; i < urls.Length; i++)
        {
            tasks[i] = FetchDataAsync(urls[i]);
        }

        var results = await Task.WhenAll(tasks);
        foreach (var result in results)
        {
            Console.WriteLine(result);
        }
    }
```

```
static        async        Task<string>
FetchDataAsync(string url)
    {
        using (HttpClient client = new
HttpClient())
        {
            string    result    =    await
client.GetStringAsync(url);
            return result;
        }
    }
}
```

Explanation:

- o   `FetchDataAsync()` is an asynchronous method that fetches the content of a URL.
- o   In `Main()`, we create a list of tasks, each calling `FetchDataAsync()` for different URLs.
- o   `Task.WhenAll()` waits for all tasks to complete, and the results are printed once all URLs have been fetched.

4. **Use Cases for async/await in C#**:

- o   **I/O-Bound Tasks**: Asynchronous programming in C# is excellent for scenarios that involve long-running I/O operations, such as querying

124

databases, making HTTP requests, or reading large files.

- o **Parallel Processing**: C# async programming can also be used in parallel with `Task.WhenAll()` to run multiple tasks concurrently and efficiently.

Real-World Use Cases for Asynchronous Design

1. **Web Crawling and Data Collection**:
   - o In a web crawling application, you need to send hundreds or thousands of requests to different websites to gather data. Asynchronous programming allows you to make these requests concurrently, reducing the total time spent crawling.
   - o **Python Example**: Using `asyncio` and `aiohttp` to send HTTP requests concurrently.
   - o **C# Example**: Using `async/await` with `HttpClient` to fetch data from multiple URLs concurrently.

2. **Real-Time Chat Applications**:
   - o Real-time chat applications need to handle thousands of simultaneous connections, making asynchronous programming crucial. By using asynchronous techniques, chat messages can be sent and received concurrently without blocking other users.

- o **Python Example**: Using `asyncio` with WebSockets to create a non-blocking chat server.
- o **C# Example**: Using `async/await` with SignalR to build real-time, event-driven chat systems.

3. **High-Performance APIs**:

- o APIs that need to handle high traffic can benefit from asynchronous programming by processing multiple requests concurrently. This allows the API to handle more requests without blocking and provides faster response times.
- o **Python Example**: Building an asynchronous API with `asyncio` and `FastAPI` to handle multiple requests simultaneously.
- o **C# Example**: Using `async/await` in ASP.NET Core to build high-performance APIs that can handle many concurrent requests without blocking.

4. **File Processing**:

- o If your application involves large file uploads, downloads, or transformations, asynchronous programming can prevent the UI from freezing while the files are being processed. This ensures a smooth user experience even when performing time-consuming tasks.
- o **Python Example**: Using `asyncio` for background file processing tasks.

○ **C# Example**: Using `async`/`await` to handle file uploads and downloads without blocking the UI thread.

In this chapter, we covered the importance of concurrency and parallelism in enterprise applications, discussed asynchronous programming techniques in Python (`asyncio`) and C# (`async`/`await`), and explored real-world use cases where asynchronous design significantly improves performance and user experience. By adopting asynchronous programming, you can ensure that your applications remain responsive, scalable, and efficient even under heavy loads.

CHAPTER 12

ERROR HANDLING AND DEBUGGING TECHNIQUES

Effective error handling and debugging are essential components of building reliable, maintainable cross-platform applications. When developing across multiple platforms, the complexity of errors and debugging challenges increases due to differences in operating systems, environments, and frameworks. In this chapter, we will explore strategies for error handling in both Python and C#, debugging tools and techniques, and common issues in cross-platform applications with their solutions.

Effective Error Handling Strategies in Python and C#

Python Error Handling Strategies:

1. **Use of Try-Except Blocks**:
   - o In Python, exceptions are handled using `try-except` blocks. These blocks allow you to catch errors and handle them appropriately, rather than letting the application crash.
   - o **Basic Example**:

```python
Copy
try:
    value = int(input("Enter a number: "))
except ValueError:
    print("Invalid input! Please enter a valid integer.")
```

- **Explanation**: This block catches the `ValueError` if the user enters non-numeric input and prints a friendly error message instead of crashing the program.

2. **Using `finally` for Cleanup**:
   - The `finally` block is used to ensure that cleanup code (such as closing files or network connections) runs regardless of whether an exception occurred or not.
   - **Example**:

```python
Copy
try:
    file = open("data.txt", "r")
    # Perform file operations
except FileNotFoundError:
    print("File not found!")
finally:
```

```
file.close()   # Ensure the file
is closed
```

3. **Custom Exceptions**:
   - You can create custom exceptions in Python by subclassing the `Exception` class. This allows you to define specific error types for your application.
   - **Example**:

```python
Copy
class CustomError(Exception):
    pass

try:
    raise CustomError("This is a
custom error!")
except CustomError as e:
    print(f"Caught an error: {e}")
```

4. **Logging Errors**:
   - Python's `logging` module is a powerful tool for tracking and recording errors. You can configure different logging levels (e.g., DEBUG, INFO, ERROR) and log messages to a file for later analysis.
   - **Example**:

```python
python
Copy
import logging

logging.basicConfig(filename="app.l
og", level=logging.ERROR)
try:
    x = 10 / 0
except ZeroDivisionError:
    logging.error("Attempted
division by zero.")
```

C# Error Handling Strategies:

1. Try-Catch Blocks:

- In C#, exceptions are handled with `try-catch` blocks, similar to Python. C# also provides the `finally` block for cleanup.
- **Basic Example**:

```csharp
csharp
Copy
try
{
    int           value           =
int.Parse(Console.ReadLine());
}
catch (FormatException)
{
```

```
        Console.WriteLine("Invalid
input!    Please    enter    a    valid
number.");
        }
```

2. **Using Multiple Catch Blocks**:

   o C# allows you to catch multiple exception types in a single `try-catch` structure. You can also use specific exception classes to handle particular error cases.

   o **Example**:

```csharp
Copy
try
{
    var        fileContent        =
File.ReadAllText("file.txt");
}
catch (FileNotFoundException ex)
{
    Console.WriteLine($"File      not
found: {ex.Message}");
}
catch    (UnauthorizedAccessException
ex)
{
    Console.WriteLine($"Access
denied: {ex.Message}");
```

```
}
```

3. **Custom Exceptions**:
   - Like Python, C# allows you to create custom exceptions by subclassing the `Exception` class.
   - **Example**:

```csharp
Copy
public class CustomException :
Exception
{
    public CustomException(string
message) : base(message) { }
}

try
{
    throw new CustomException("This
is a custom exception.");
}
catch (CustomException ex)
{
    Console.WriteLine(ex.Message);
}
```

4. **Using `finally` for Cleanup**:

o The `finally` block in C# ensures that cleanup code is executed, such as closing database connections or releasing file handles.

o **Example**:

```csharp
Copy
try
{
    var file = File.Open("data.txt",
FileMode.Open);
}
catch (FileNotFoundException ex)
{
    Console.WriteLine(ex.Message);
}
finally
{
    Console.WriteLine("File
operation finished.");
}
```

Debugging Tools and Techniques for Both Environments

Python Debugging Tools:

1. **Built-in Debugger (pdb)**:

   o Python's `pdb` (Python Debugger) is a command-line tool that allows you to set breakpoints,

134

inspect variables, and step through code line by line.

o **Usage**:

```python
Copy
import pdb
x = 5
y = 10
pdb.set_trace()    # Execution will
pause here
result = x + y
print(result)
```

2. **Visual Debugging with IDEs**:

   o IDEs like PyCharm or Visual Studio Code offer visual debugging tools that make it easier to set breakpoints, step through code, inspect variables, and manage the flow of execution.

3. **Logging**:

   o Logging in Python can be a more practical alternative for debugging, especially for production environments. Python's `logging` module provides different log levels and allows you to track the flow of execution.

C# Debugging Tools:

1. **Visual Studio Debugger**:
   - Visual Studio offers a powerful graphical debugger that allows you to step through your code, inspect variables, set breakpoints, and track the call stack.
   - **Features**:
     - **Breakpoints**: Pause execution at specific lines of code.
     - **Watch Variables**: Track the value of variables while debugging.
     - **Call Stack**: View the chain of method calls leading to the current line of execution.
     - **Immediate Window**: Evaluate expressions while debugging.

2. **Console Debugging with `System.Diagnostics`**:
   - You can use `System.Diagnostics` to print out debug information, such as timestamps and variable values, to the console or a log file.
   - **Example**:

```csharp
Copy
using System.Diagnostics;

Debug.WriteLine("This is a debug message");
```

3. **Unit Testing Frameworks**:

   o In C#, you can use unit testing frameworks like NUnit or MSTest to write and execute tests, ensuring that the code behaves as expected and helping you find bugs earlier in the development cycle.

Common Issues and Solutions in Cross-Platform Applications

1. **Platform-Specific Bugs**:

   o **Issue**: Cross-platform applications often face bugs that occur on specific operating systems due to differences in system configurations, file paths, or APIs.

   o **Solution**: Use platform-specific code to handle variations in file paths, libraries, and system APIs. In C#, use `#if` preprocessor directives, and in Python, use the `platform` module to determine the operating system.

2. **File System Issues**:

   o **Issue**: File system paths may differ across platforms (e.g., Windows uses backslashes, while Linux and macOS use forward slashes).

   o **Solution**: Use platform-agnostic libraries, such as Python's `os.path` or C#'s `Path.Combine()`, to construct file paths in a cross-platform way.

3. **Concurrency and Threading Issues**:
   - o **Issue**: Asynchronous operations can sometimes lead to race conditions or deadlocks, particularly in complex multi-threaded environments.
   - o **Solution**: Use thread-safe data structures, avoid shared mutable state, and carefully manage access to shared resources. For debugging threading issues, both Python and C# provide thread debugging tools that allow you to view thread states and detect deadlocks.

4. **Cross-Platform Dependencies**:
   - o **Issue**: Some libraries or dependencies may not be fully supported across all platforms, leading to compatibility issues.
   - o **Solution**: Use cross-platform libraries or APIs that are designed to work on multiple operating systems. Ensure that you test your application on all target platforms to catch issues early. In C#, .NET Core provides a large set of cross-platform libraries.

5. **Network and API Integration Problems**:
   - o **Issue**: Cross-platform applications that rely on network communication or third-party APIs can encounter differences in how requests are handled across platforms, such as inconsistent network latency or API rate limiting.

○ **Solution**: Implement retries, timeouts, and error handling when making network requests. Use async programming to avoid blocking the main thread while waiting for network responses.

In this chapter, we covered effective error handling strategies in Python and C#, debugging tools and techniques for both environments, and common issues in cross-platform applications. By implementing proper error handling, leveraging debugging tools, and addressing common cross-platform issues, you can create more robust, maintainable applications that work seamlessly across different platforms.

CHAPTER 13

CLOUD INTEGRATION FOR ENTERPRISE SOLUTIONS

Cloud computing has revolutionized how enterprises build, deploy, and scale their applications. By leveraging cloud platforms, organizations can access a broad range of services, including storage, messaging, and compute power, without the need for extensive on-premise infrastructure. In this chapter, we will explore how to integrate cloud platforms (AWS, Azure, and Google Cloud) with enterprise solutions, focusing on cloud storage, messaging services, and compute resources. We'll also cover real-world examples of how cross-platform apps can leverage these services to improve performance, scalability, and functionality.

Using Cloud Platforms (AWS, Azure, Google Cloud)

Amazon Web Services (AWS):

AWS is one of the most popular cloud platforms, offering a wide range of services for compute, storage, databases, and machine learning. It provides a highly scalable and flexible environment for deploying enterprise applications.

1. **AWS Services for Enterprise Solutions**:
   - **Amazon EC2**: Elastic Compute Cloud (EC2) provides scalable compute capacity, allowing you to run virtual machines on-demand. EC2 is essential for hosting web servers, APIs, and applications.
   - **Amazon S3**: Simple Storage Service (S3) is an object storage service for storing and retrieving large amounts of data. It's commonly used for storing files, backups, and other unstructured data.
   - **Amazon RDS**: Relational Database Service (RDS) allows you to run relational databases like MySQL, PostgreSQL, or SQL Server in the cloud with automated backups, scaling, and patching.
   - **Amazon SNS**: Simple Notification Service (SNS) is a messaging service for sending notifications or messages to distributed systems or services.

2. **Integration with Cross-Platform Apps**:
   - Use the **AWS SDK** for Python (`boto3`) or C# to integrate AWS services into your applications. The SDK allows you to interact with AWS

resources such as S3 for file storage or EC2 for compute power.

Microsoft Azure:

Azure is a cloud platform by Microsoft that provides a comprehensive set of services for building, deploying, and managing applications. It is well-integrated with the Microsoft ecosystem, making it a strong choice for enterprise solutions.

1. **Azure Services for Enterprise Solutions**:
   o **Azure Virtual Machines**: Similar to AWS EC2, Azure Virtual Machines provide scalable compute resources for running applications in the cloud.
   o **Azure Blob Storage**: Azure's equivalent to S3, Blob Storage is used to store unstructured data like images, videos, and documents.
   o **Azure SQL Database**: A fully managed relational database service that supports SQL Server, MySQL, and PostgreSQL databases, offering high availability and scalability.
   o **Azure Service Bus**: Azure's messaging service allows you to decouple applications and services, providing reliable message delivery between distributed systems.

2. **Integration with Cross-Platform Apps**:

   o Use **Azure SDKs** for Python (`azure-sdk`) or C# to integrate your applications with Azure services. This allows cross-platform apps to leverage Azure's compute, storage, and messaging capabilities.

Google Cloud Platform (GCP):

Google Cloud offers robust cloud services for building, deploying, and scaling enterprise applications. Google Cloud is known for its powerful machine learning, data analytics, and compute services.

1. **GCP Services for Enterprise Solutions**:

   o **Google Compute Engine**: Google's equivalent to EC2, providing virtual machines to run applications and services in the cloud.

   o **Google Cloud Storage**: An object storage service similar to AWS S3, used to store large amounts of unstructured data.

   o **Google Cloud SQL**: A fully-managed relational database service that supports MySQL, PostgreSQL, and SQL Server databases.

   o **Google Pub/Sub**: A messaging service for event-driven systems, allowing applications to send and receive messages asynchronously.

143

2. **Integration with Cross-Platform Apps**:

   o Use the **Google Cloud SDK** for Python or C# to integrate Google Cloud services into your application. You can interact with services like Cloud Storage for file management or Pub/Sub for messaging.

Cloud Storage, Messaging Services, and Compute

Cloud platforms provide a range of services that are essential for enterprise applications, including storage, messaging, and compute. Let's explore these services in more detail and how they can be leveraged for cross-platform applications.

Cloud Storage:

Cloud storage allows businesses to store and retrieve data over the internet. It is an essential component of most modern enterprise applications.

1. **AWS S3, Azure Blob Storage, and Google Cloud Storage**:

   o These services allow you to store large volumes of unstructured data, such as images, videos, and backups. They provide highly durable and scalable storage solutions.

   o **Integration with Cross-Platform Apps**:

- In Python, use the `boto3` library to interact with S3, `azure-storage-blob` to interact with Azure Blob Storage, or `google-cloud-storage` for Google Cloud.
- In C#, use the **AWS SDK for .NET**, **Azure.Storage.Blobs** library, or **Google.Cloud.Storage.V1** library.

2. **Use Cases**:

   o **Backup and Recovery**: Cloud storage is ideal for securely storing backups and enabling disaster recovery for cross-platform applications.

   o **File Sharing**: Cross-platform applications can use cloud storage to upload, download, and share files across different devices and operating systems.

Cloud Messaging Services:

Cloud messaging services enable communication between distributed systems and decouple different components of an application. These services are critical in event-driven architectures and microservices.

1. **AWS SNS, Azure Service Bus, and Google Pub/Sub**:

- o These messaging services provide reliable message delivery for event-driven systems, real-time updates, and decoupled communication between services.
- o **Integration with Cross-Platform Apps**:
  - In Python, you can use `boto3` for AWS SNS, `azure-servicebus` for Azure Service Bus, or `google-cloud-pubsub` for Google Pub/Sub.
  - In C#, use the **AWS SDK for .NET**, **Azure.Messaging.ServiceBus** library, or **Google.Cloud.PubSub.V1** library.

2. **Use Cases**:
   - o **Event-Driven Systems**: Messaging services can be used to notify other systems when specific events occur, such as a new user registration or a payment transaction.
   - o **Real-Time Communication**: Cloud messaging is often used in chat applications, live notifications, and real-time updates in enterprise solutions.

Cloud Compute Services:

Cloud compute services allow you to run applications on virtual machines (VMs) or serverless platforms. They provide the computing resources needed for processing tasks, running APIs, or hosting applications.

1. **AWS EC2, Azure Virtual Machines, and Google Compute Engine**:
   - These services provide scalable compute resources that can run a variety of applications. With EC2, Virtual Machines, and Compute Engine, you can provision instances to match your application's needs, from small workloads to large-scale systems.
   - **Serverless Options**: All three platforms offer serverless computing solutions (AWS Lambda, Azure Functions, and Google Cloud Functions) that automatically scale to handle increasing traffic.

2. **Integration with Cross-Platform Apps**:
   - For Python and C#, you can interact with compute services using the respective cloud SDKs, enabling you to deploy, manage, and scale your applications across platforms.

3. **Use Cases**:
   - **Web Hosting**: Host your web applications or APIs on cloud compute instances.
   - **Microservices**: Use serverless compute services for microservices architectures, where each

function or service can scale independently based on demand.

Examples of Integrating Cloud Services with Cross-Platform Apps

Example 1: Cross-Platform File Management Application (Python + AWS S3):

- **Scenario**: A file management application allows users to upload and share files across multiple devices (Windows, macOS, Linux).
- **Cloud Integration**: The application uses AWS S3 for file storage, where files are uploaded from the user's local machine and stored in the cloud. Users can download and share files from any device.
- **Python Integration**: Using the boto3 library, the Python application interacts with S3 to upload and retrieve files.
- **Code Snippet** (Python):

```python
Copy
import boto3
s3 = boto3.client('s3')
def upload_file(file_name, bucket_name):
    s3.upload_file(file_name, bucket_name,
file_name)
```

Example 2: Cross-Platform Messaging Application (C# + Azure Service Bus):

- **Scenario**: A cross-platform enterprise messaging app allows users to send real-time messages across multiple platforms (Windows, iOS, Android).
- **Cloud Integration**: The app uses Azure Service Bus to handle message queues. Messages are sent asynchronously between clients, enabling real-time communication.
- **C# Integration**: The C# application uses the **Azure.Messaging.ServiceBus** library to send and receive messages from Azure Service Bus.
- **Code Snippet** (C#):

```csharp
Copy
using Azure.Messaging.ServiceBus;

ServiceBusClient client = new ServiceBusClient("YourConnectionString");
ServiceBusSender sender = client.CreateSender("yourQueueName");

ServiceBusMessage message = new ServiceBusMessage("Hello, world!");
await sender.SendMessageAsync(message);
```

Example 3: Cross-Platform Task Management Application (Python + Google Cloud Functions):

- **Scenario**: A task management application enables users to create, update, and track tasks from multiple devices.
- **Cloud Integration**: The backend logic for handling tasks is implemented as serverless functions using Google Cloud Functions. Each task action (create, update, delete) triggers a cloud function.
- **Python Integration**: The Python application calls Google Cloud Functions via HTTP requests, using the `google-cloud` SDK to interact with the cloud.
- **Code Snippet** (Python):

```python
Copy
import google.auth
from google.auth.transport.requests import Request
from google.cloud import functions_v1

def call_cloud_function():
    client = functions_v1.CloudFunctionsServiceClient()
    response = client.call_function(name="projects/your-
```

```
project-id/locations/us-
central1/functions/your-function-name")
    print(response.result())
```

In this chapter, we covered how cloud platforms (AWS, Azure, and Google Cloud) can be integrated into cross-platform enterprise applications. We explored cloud storage, messaging services, and compute resources, and demonstrated how these services can enhance application performance and scalability. Through examples, we also highlighted how to use cloud services in Python and C# applications to build robust, cross-platform enterprise solutions.

151

CHAPTER 14

MICROSERVICES ARCHITECTURE WITH PYTHON AND C#

In modern enterprise applications, microservices architecture has become a dominant design pattern due to its flexibility, scalability, and ability to enable continuous delivery. Microservices decompose a complex application into smaller, loosely coupled services, each of which can be developed, deployed, and scaled independently. In this chapter, we will explore the concept of microservices, how to implement microservices with Python and C#, and provide real-world enterprise examples that demonstrate how microservices can be successfully implemented.

Introduction to Microservices

What Are Microservices?

Microservices architecture is a design pattern where a large application is broken down into smaller, independent services that focus on specific business functionalities. Each microservice is self-contained, runs in its own process, and communicates with other microservices via lightweight protocols, typically over HTTP/REST or messaging queues.

The key characteristics of microservices include:

1. **Modularity**: Each microservice is a small, independent unit of functionality (e.g., user authentication, payment processing, or order management).

2. **Independent Deployment**: Each microservice can be deployed, updated, or scaled independently, enabling continuous integration and delivery.

3. **Autonomy**: Microservices operate independently, allowing teams to work on different services in parallel without affecting other services.

4. **Fault Isolation**: Because microservices are decoupled, failures in one service don't directly affect other services.

5. **Scalability**: Microservices can be scaled independently, meaning you can allocate resources to the services that require them the most.

Benefits of Microservices:

- **Scalability**: Individual services can be scaled based on demand, without needing to scale the entire application.

- **Flexibility**: You can use different programming languages, databases, and frameworks for each microservice.
- **Faster Development**: Teams can work on separate services in parallel, reducing development time.
- **Fault Isolation**: The failure of one service does not necessarily bring down the entire application.
- **Easier Maintenance**: Small, isolated services are easier to manage, test, and deploy.

Challenges of Microservices:

- **Complexity**: Microservices introduce complexity in managing inter-service communication, versioning, and deployment pipelines.
- **Data Consistency**: Ensuring data consistency across distributed services can be tricky, especially in eventual consistency scenarios.
- **Inter-service Communication**: Microservices often rely on APIs or messaging systems for communication, which introduces latency and can become a bottleneck if not designed well.

How to Implement Microservices with Python and C#

Implementing Microservices with Python:

Python is a flexible and powerful language that is well-suited for building microservices. It offers various frameworks and tools for building and managing microservices, including Flask, FastAPI, and Django REST Framework. These frameworks allow developers to create lightweight and fast APIs that can be used as microservices.

1. **Flask and FastAPI**:
    - **Flask** is a micro-framework for building web applications. It is lightweight, flexible, and ideal for creating simple, RESTful APIs.
    - **FastAPI** is another Python framework designed for building APIs quickly. It is asynchronous, making it ideal for high-performance microservices that handle many simultaneous requests.

2. **Creating a Simple Microservice in Python with Flask**:
    - **Step 1: Install Flask**:

    ```bash
    Copy
    pip install Flask
    ```

    - **Step 2: Create a simple RESTful service**:

    ```python
    ```

```
Copy
from flask import Flask, jsonify

app = Flask(__name__)

@app.route('/api/v1/hello',
methods=['GET'])
def hello():
    return        jsonify({"message":
"Hello, Microservice!"})

if __name__ == '__main__':
    app.run(debug=True)
```

- o This simple Flask application serves as a microservice with a single endpoint that returns a "Hello, Microservice!" message.

3. **Asynchronous Microservice with FastAPI**:
   - o **Step 1: Install FastAPI and Uvicorn** (ASGI server):

```bash
Copy
pip install fastapi uvicorn
```

   - o **Step 2: Create an asynchronous microservice**:

```python
Copy
```

156

```
from fastapi import FastAPI

app = FastAPI()

@app.get("/api/v1/hello")
async def hello():
    return    {"message":    "Hello,
Microservice with FastAPI!"}

if __name__ == "__main__":
    import uvicorn
    uvicorn.run(app, host="0.0.0.0",
port=8000)
```

- o FastAPI makes it easy to write asynchronous endpoints, which is essential for handling high-concurrency in microservices.

4. **Inter-service Communication**:
   - o **REST APIs**: Python microservices can communicate via HTTP using REST APIs. You can use libraries like `requests` to make HTTP requests between services.
   - o **Message Brokers**: For asynchronous communication, Python microservices can use message brokers like RabbitMQ or Kafka for inter-service messaging.

Implementing Microservices with C# (ASP.NET Core):

C# and ASP.NET Core are widely used in enterprise environments for building scalable, maintainable microservices. ASP.NET Core provides excellent support for creating APIs, and it is highly performant, making it ideal for microservices.

1. **Creating a Simple Microservice in C# with ASP.NET Core**:
    - **Step 1: Create an ASP.NET Core Web API Project**:
        - Use the Visual Studio template or the .NET CLI to create a new Web API project:

```bash
Copy
dotnet new webapi -n MyMicroservice
cd MyMicroservice
```

    - **Step 2: Define a simple endpoint**: In `Controllers/WeatherForecastController.cs`, replace the default code with:

```csharp
Copy
using Microsoft.AspNetCore.Mvc;
using System.Collections.Generic;
```

158

```
namespace MyMicroservice.Controllers
{
    [ApiController]
    [Route("api/[controller]")]
    public class HelloController :
ControllerBase
    {
        [HttpGet]
        public IActionResult Get()
        {
            return Ok(new { message
= "Hello, Microservice!" });
        }
    }
}
```

2. **Asynchronous Microservice with C#**:

   o In C#, asynchronous methods are created using async and await. This is useful when building microservices that need to handle high I/O loads, such as database access or calling external APIs.

   o **Example**:

```
csharp
Copy
public   async   Task<IActionResult>
GetWeatherAsync()
{
```

```
      var   weatherData   =   await
_weatherService.GetWeatherDataAsync
();
      return Ok(weatherData);
}
```

3. **Inter-service Communication**:

   o **REST APIs**: Like Python, C# microservices often communicate via REST APIs. You can use `HttpClient` to make HTTP requests to other services.

   o **Message Queues**: C# microservices can also use messaging services like RabbitMQ or Azure Service Bus for asynchronous communication.

4. **Dockerizing Microservices**:

   o Both Python and C# microservices can be packaged in Docker containers, making it easier to deploy and scale them in a cloud or on-premise environment.

Real-World Enterprise Examples of Microservices Implementation

Example 1: E-Commerce Platform with Python Microservices:

- **Scenario**: An e-commerce company needs to break down its monolithic application into smaller,

160

independent services such as product management, user authentication, and order processing.

- **Solution**:
    - o **User Authentication Service**: A Python microservice using **Flask** to handle user login, registration, and session management.
    - o **Product Catalog Service**: A Python microservice using **FastAPI** to manage the product catalog and provide product information via REST APIs.
    - o **Order Processing Service**: A Python microservice that handles order creation, payment processing, and shipment tracking, communicating with external payment gateways via APIs.

The Python microservices communicate using RESTful APIs, and inter-service communication is handled asynchronously using **RabbitMQ** for event-driven interactions (e.g., sending notifications when an order is shipped).

Example 2: Financial Services Application with C# Microservices:

- **Scenario**: A financial institution wants to build a scalable and reliable system to manage customer accounts, transactions, and reporting.
- **Solution**:
  - **Account Service**: A C# microservice built with **ASP.NET Core** that manages customer account information.
  - **Transaction Service**: A C# microservice that handles financial transactions, such as deposits, withdrawals, and transfers.
  - **Reporting Service**: A C# microservice responsible for generating financial reports, querying transaction data, and exporting reports to PDF or Excel.

The microservices communicate via REST APIs, and for high-performance scenarios, they use **Azure Service Bus** for messaging. The microservices are deployed in containers and orchestrated using **Kubernetes** for scalability and fault tolerance.

Example 3: Social Media Platform with Hybrid Python and C# Microservices:

- **Scenario**: A social media platform needs to scale its services across different regions, with different teams handling features like user profiles, posts, notifications, and analytics.

- **Solution**:
    - o **User Profile Service (Python)**: A microservice built with **Flask** to handle user profile creation, updates, and retrieval.
    - o **Post Management Service (C#)**: A microservice built with **ASP.NET Core** to manage posts, comments, and likes.
    - o **Notification Service (Python)**: A Python microservice that sends push notifications to users when there are new posts, comments, or likes.
    - o **Analytics Service (C#)**: A microservice that analyzes user activity and provides data insights, built using **C#** and **Azure**.

These microservices communicate via REST APIs and integrate with an internal **message queue** for event-driven architecture. They are deployed in **Docker containers** and use **Kubernetes** for orchestration.

In this chapter, we covered the fundamental concepts of microservices, explored how to implement them using Python and C#, and discussed real-world examples of enterprise applications that use microservices. By adopting a microservices architecture, businesses can improve scalability, fault isolation, and flexibility, enabling faster development cycles and better overall system performance.

CHAPTER 15

CONTINUOUS INTEGRATION AND CONTINUOUS DEPLOYMENT (CI/CD)

In modern software development, Continuous Integration (CI) and Continuous Deployment (CD) are critical practices that ensure code changes are integrated, tested, and deployed efficiently and reliably. These practices are especially important for cross-platform solutions, as they help teams maintain consistency and quality across different platforms. In this chapter, we'll explore the concepts of CI/CD pipelines, how to automate builds and deployments with popular tools like Jenkins, GitLab, and Azure DevOps, and provide real-world examples of CI/CD workflows in action.

CI/CD Pipelines for Cross-Platform Solutions

What is Continuous Integration (CI)?

Continuous Integration refers to the practice of automatically integrating code changes into a shared repository frequently, multiple times a day. The goal is to detect issues early by running automated tests on every change. CI helps ensure that new code is always integrated smoothly and that the software is consistently in a deployable state.

What is Continuous Deployment (CD)?

Continuous Deployment refers to the process of automatically deploying code to production after passing all tests in the CI pipeline. This allows for frequent releases, making it possible to deliver new features and bug fixes quickly and reliably.

Why is CI/CD Important for Cross-Platform Solutions?

For cross-platform solutions, CI/CD pipelines provide several benefits:

- **Consistency**: Automated pipelines ensure that the application is built and deployed the same way across all platforms, whether it's Windows, macOS, or Linux.
- **Faster Development**: By automating repetitive tasks like builds, tests, and deployments, development teams can focus more on writing code and less on manual deployment steps.

- **Reliability**: CI/CD ensures that bugs and issues are identified early, reducing the chances of introducing errors in production.
- **Scalability**: CI/CD pipelines can easily scale with the growing complexity of cross-platform solutions, handling more builds, tests, and deployments across multiple environments.

Automating Builds and Deployments with Jenkins, GitLab, and Azure DevOps

Jenkins:

Jenkins is one of the most widely used open-source automation servers. It supports continuous integration and continuous delivery, making it a go-to tool for automating builds, tests, and deployments.

1. **Setting Up a Jenkins Pipeline for Cross-Platform Solutions**:
   - **Step 1: Install Jenkins**: Install Jenkins on a server or use Jenkins as a cloud service.
   - **Step 2: Create a Jenkinsfile**: A Jenkinsfile defines the CI/CD pipeline and its stages (e.g., build, test, deploy). The Jenkinsfile is typically stored in the repository and can

define steps for building, testing, and deploying cross-platform applications.

- **Example Jenkinsfile** (for a Python and C# project):

```groovy
Copy
pipeline {
    agent any
    stages {
        stage('Build') {
            steps {
                script {
                    //
Example: Build Python and C#
apps
                    sh 'python
-m unittest discover'
                    bat
'dotnet build MyApp.sln'
                }
            }
        }
        stage('Test') {
            steps {
                script {
                    //      Run
tests
```

168

```
                              sh 'pytest
tests/'
                              bat
'dotnet test MyApp.Tests'
                              }
                        }
                  }
            stage('Deploy') {
                steps {
                    script {
                        // Deploy
to staging or production
                        sh 'docker
build -t myapp .'
                        sh
'docker-compose up -d'
                    }
                }
            }
        }
    }
```

o **Step 3: Run the Pipeline**: Jenkins will automatically trigger the pipeline on each code change, running the build, tests, and deployment steps.

GitLab CI/CD:

GitLab is an integrated platform that provides source code management, CI/CD pipelines, and DevOps features. GitLab CI/CD pipelines are defined in a `.gitlab-ci.yml` file, which specifies the build, test, and deploy stages.

1. **Setting Up a GitLab CI/CD Pipeline**:
   - **Step 1: Define a GitLab Pipeline**:
     - **Example .gitlab-ci.yml**:

```yaml
Copy
stages:
  - build
  - test
  - deploy

build:
  script:
    - echo "Building Python and C# apps..."
    - python -m unittest discover
    - dotnet build MyApp.sln

test:
  script:
    - echo "Running tests..."
    - pytest tests/
    - dotnet test MyApp.Tests
```

170

```
deploy:
  script:
    - echo "Deploying to
production..."
    - docker-compose up -d
```

- o **Step 2: Run the Pipeline**: GitLab will trigger the pipeline whenever there are changes pushed to the repository, running through the defined stages.

Azure DevOps:

Azure DevOps is a set of development tools from Microsoft for automating the entire application lifecycle, including CI/CD. Azure Pipelines is the service in Azure DevOps for creating and running CI/CD pipelines.

1. **Setting Up a Pipeline in Azure DevOps**:
   - o **Step 1: Create a YAML Pipeline**: Azure DevOps pipelines can be defined in a YAML file (`azure-pipelines.yml`), similar to Jenkins and GitLab.
     - ▪ **Example azure-pipelines.yml**:

       ```
       yaml
       Copy
       ```

```yaml
trigger:
  branches:
    include:
      - main

pool:
  vmImage: 'ubuntu-latest'

steps:
  - task: UsePythonVersion@0
    inputs:
      versionSpec: '3.x'

  - script: |
      echo "Building Python and C# apps..."
      python -m unittest discover
      dotnet build MyApp.sln
    displayName: 'Build Project'

  - script: |
      echo "Running tests..."
      pytest tests/
      dotnet test MyApp.Tests
    displayName: 'Run Tests'

  - script: |
```

```
        echo    "Deploying    to
production..."
        docker-compose up -d
    displayName:         'Deploy
Project'
```

o **Step 2: Run the Pipeline**: Azure DevOps will automatically run the pipeline when changes are pushed to the `main` branch, executing the build, test, and deployment tasks.

Real-World Examples of CI/CD Workflows

Example 1: E-Commerce Application (Python + C# with AWS)

- **Scenario**: A large-scale e-commerce platform is built with Python for the backend API and C# for the frontend user interface. The platform needs to deploy updates frequently to ensure a competitive edge in the market.
- **CI/CD Workflow**:
    o **Build**: On each commit to the repository, Jenkins runs a pipeline that builds both the Python backend and the C# frontend.
    o **Test**: Automated unit and integration tests are run on both the Python API (using `pytest`) and the C# frontend (using `dotnet test`).

173

- o **Deploy**: After passing the tests, the application is packaged using Docker and deployed to AWS EC2 instances using AWS CodeDeploy.

- o **Automation**: Jenkins monitors the Git repository for changes and automatically triggers the build and deployment pipeline when new code is pushed.

Example 2: Mobile App Development (Cross-Platform with Xamarin)

- **Scenario**: A mobile app is developed using Xamarin for both Android and iOS platforms. The app needs to be tested on multiple devices and deployed to app stores regularly.

- **CI/CD Workflow**:
  - o **Build**: GitLab CI is configured to build the Xamarin app for both Android and iOS.
  - o **Test**: Automated UI and unit tests are executed for both platforms using tools like Appium (for UI testing) and NUnit (for unit testing).
  - o **Deploy**: The app is deployed to staging environments for both Android and iOS using Firebase and TestFlight. After successful testing, it is deployed to the Google Play Store and Apple App Store using Fastlane, integrated into the GitLab pipeline.

174

Example 3: Financial Services (C# with Azure DevOps)

- **Scenario**: A financial institution uses C# for developing its core services. The application needs to handle thousands of transactions per minute, and the code is frequently updated with new features and bug fixes.
- **CI/CD Workflow**:
  - **Build**: Azure DevOps is used to build the C# application on every commit to the main branch. The application is built for both cloud and on-premise environments.
  - **Test**: Unit tests, integration tests, and load tests are automatically triggered in the pipeline.
  - **Deploy**: The application is deployed to an Azure App Service for cloud-based environments, while an on-premise version is deployed using Azure DevOps Release Pipelines.
  - **Automation**: The pipeline runs automatically every time there is a change in the repository, ensuring rapid delivery and a continuous flow of updates without downtime.

In this chapter, we explored CI/CD pipelines for cross-platform solutions, focusing on how to automate builds and deployments using Jenkins, GitLab, and Azure DevOps. We also discussed real-world examples of CI/CD workflows that streamline the development and deployment processes in modern enterprise applications. By integrating CI/CD into your development process, you can ensure faster, more reliable delivery of cross-platform solutions, improving efficiency and reducing the risk of bugs in production.

CHAPTER 16

TESTING STRATEGIES FOR CROSS-PLATFORM APPLICATIONS

Testing is a critical part of software development that ensures the quality and reliability of applications. For cross-platform applications, effective testing strategies are essential to ensure that the application works consistently and correctly across various platforms. This chapter explores different types of testing, such as unit testing, integration testing, and functional testing, and how they can be implemented in both Python and C#. We will also look at using testing frameworks in Python (pytest, unittest) and C# (NUnit, xUnit) and discuss continuous testing practices.

Unit Testing, Integration Testing, and Functional Testing

1. Unit Testing:

Unit testing involves testing individual units of code in isolation to verify that they perform as expected. Each unit (usually a single function or method) is tested independently

177

from the rest of the application. Unit tests should be fast and easy to execute.

- **Purpose**: Ensure that each component of the application behaves as expected in isolation.
- **Focus**: Individual functions or methods.
- **Tools**: Testing frameworks like pytest, unittest (Python), and NUnit, xUnit (C#).

Example (Python - Unit Test):

```python
Copy
def add(x, y):
    return x + y


# Unit test using unittest
import unittest

class TestAddition(unittest.TestCase):
    def test_add(self):
        self.assertEqual(add(1, 2), 3)
        self.assertEqual(add(-1, 1), 0)

if __name__ == "__main__":
    unittest.main()
```

2. Integration Testing:

Integration testing focuses on verifying the interactions between different components or modules of the application. The goal is to ensure that the integrated components work together as expected. This type of testing is particularly important for cross-platform applications, where different components may behave differently on different platforms.

- **Purpose**: Ensure that different parts of the application work together properly.
- **Focus**: Interactions between modules, services, and external systems (e.g., databases, APIs).
- **Tools**: pytest, unittest (Python), NUnit, xUnit (C#).

Example (C# - Integration Test):

```csharp
Copy
public class DatabaseService
{
    public string GetData(int id)
    {
        // Simulate fetching data from a database
        if (id == 1)
            return "Data for ID 1";
        else
            return "Not found";
    }
}
```

```
public class DatabaseServiceTest
{
    [Fact]
    public void TestGetData()
    {
        var service = new DatabaseService();
        var result = service.GetData(1);
        Assert.Equal("Data for ID 1", result);
    }
}
```

3. Functional Testing:

Functional testing evaluates the overall functionality of the application by simulating real user scenarios. It checks whether the application meets its business requirements and works correctly on all platforms. This is often performed manually or using automated UI testing tools.

- **Purpose**: Verify that the application functions as expected from the user's perspective.
- **Focus**: End-to-end application behavior.
- **Tools**: Selenium, Appium (for UI testing), pytest, and unittest (Python), NUnit, xUnit (C#).

Example (Python - Functional Test with Selenium):

```python
Copy
from selenium import webdriver

def test_login():
    driver = webdriver.Chrome()
    driver.get("https://example.com/login")

driver.find_element_by_id("username").send_keys
("user")

driver.find_element_by_id("password").send_keys
("password")

driver.find_element_by_id("login_button").click
()
    assert "Dashboard" in driver.title
    driver.quit()
```

Using Testing Frameworks in Python (pytest, unittest) and C# (NUnit, xUnit)

Testing Frameworks in Python:

1. **pytest**:

   o pytest is a popular Python testing framework known for its simplicity and scalability. It allows for writing clean, readable tests and supports fixtures, parameterization, and other advanced features.

o **Example**:

```python
Copy
import pytest

def add(x, y):
    return x + y

# Unit test using pytest
def test_add():
    assert add(1, 2) == 3
    assert add(-1, 1) == 0
```

2. **unittest**:

o unittest is a built-in testing framework in Python that follows the xUnit style for writing tests. It is more verbose than pytest but is useful for developers who prefer a more structured approach.

o **Example**:

```python
Copy
import unittest
```

```
class
TestAddition(unittest.TestCase):
    def test_add(self):
        self.assertEqual(add(1,   2),
3)
        self.assertEqual(add(-1, 1),
0)

if __name__ == "__main__":
    unittest.main()
```

Testing Frameworks in C#:

1. NUnit:

- ○ NUnit is a widely used testing framework for C# that follows the xUnit pattern and provides powerful assertions and test runners.
- ○ **Example**:

```csharp
Copy
using NUnit.Framework;

public class TestAddition
{
    [Test]
    public void TestAdd()
    {
```

183

```
            Assert.AreEqual(3,      Add(1,
2));
            Assert.AreEqual(0,      Add(-1,
1));
        }

        public int Add(int x,  int y)
        {
            return x + y;
        }
    }
```

2. **xUnit**:

    o   xUnit is another popular testing framework in
        C# that is lightweight and optimized for parallel
        test execution.

    o   **Example**:

```
csharp
Copy
using Xunit;

public class TestAddition
{
    [Fact]
    public void TestAdd()
    {
        Assert.Equal(3, Add(1, 2));
        Assert.Equal(0, Add(-1, 1));
```

```
        }

        public int Add(int x, int y)
        {
                return x + y;
        }
    }
```

Continuous Testing Practices

Continuous testing is the practice of running automated tests continuously throughout the software development lifecycle to ensure code quality and catch issues early. Integrating continuous testing into your CI/CD pipeline is crucial for maintaining the reliability of cross-platform applications.

1. Integration with CI/CD Pipelines:

- **Automated Testing**: Integrate unit tests, integration tests, and functional tests into your CI/CD pipelines to ensure that every change is automatically tested before being deployed.
- **Test Coverage**: Ensure comprehensive test coverage by running tests across all critical application features and platforms. Tools like `pytest-cov` (for Python) and `coverlet` (for C#) can be used to measure code coverage.

185

2. Parallel Test Execution:

- To speed up testing, especially for large applications, run tests in parallel across multiple environments. Many CI/CD tools, including Jenkins, GitLab CI, and Azure DevOps, support parallel test execution to reduce build times.

3. Cross-Platform Testing:

- For cross-platform applications, it's essential to run tests on multiple operating systems (Windows, macOS, Linux) and device types (mobile, desktop). Tools like Selenium Grid, BrowserStack, and Sauce Labs provide cloud-based testing services that enable testing across different platforms and browsers.

4. Test Automation Frameworks:

- **Python**: Use frameworks like **pytest** or **unittest** for running automated tests, and integrate with tools like **Selenium** for browser-based testing and **Appium** for mobile testing.
- **C#**: Leverage tools like **NUnit** or **xUnit** for unit testing and integrate them with **Selenium** or **Appium** for UI testing.

5. Continuous Feedback:

- Provide continuous feedback to developers by sending notifications of test results via email, Slack, or other communication channels. This ensures that issues are identified early, and developers can quickly address them.

Example (GitLab CI with Continuous Testing):

```yaml
Copy
stages:
  - build
  - test
  - deploy

test:
  script:
    - pytest --maxfail=1 --disable-warnings -q
    - dotnet test MyApp.Tests --logger "trx;LogFileName=test_results.trx"
  artifacts:
    paths:
      - test_results.trx
    expire_in: 1 week
```

This CI pipeline runs tests on both the Python and C# parts of the application, and the test results are saved as artifacts for further analysis.

In this chapter, we covered various testing strategies for cross-platform applications, including unit testing, integration testing, and functional testing. We discussed how to use popular testing frameworks like pytest, unittest (Python), and NUnit, xUnit (C#) to implement these tests. Additionally, we explored continuous testing practices, including how to integrate tests into CI/CD pipelines to ensure consistent quality and reliability throughout the software development lifecycle. By adopting these testing strategies, teams can build and maintain robust cross-platform applications that meet high standards of performance and reliability.

CHAPTER 17

HANDLING CROSS-PLATFORM COMPATIBILITY ISSUES

Developing cross-platform applications is essential in today's software development landscape, but it comes with its own set of challenges. One of the most common challenges is ensuring that the application behaves consistently across different platforms (Windows, macOS, Linux, Android, iOS). In this chapter, we'll address some of the most common issues developers face when building cross-platform apps, provide strategies for debugging and testing cross-platform compatibility, and showcase real-world examples of how to overcome compatibility challenges.

Addressing Common Issues When Developing Cross-Platform Apps

1. **File System Differences**:
   - o **Issue**: Different operating systems handle file paths and file systems differently. For example, Windows uses backslashes (\) in file paths, while macOS and Linux use forward slashes (/).

o **Solution**: Always use platform-agnostic libraries to handle file paths. In Python, the `os.path` module or `pathlib` module can abstract away platform-specific differences. In C#, the `Path.Combine()` method in the `System.IO` namespace helps ensure that paths are constructed correctly, regardless of the platform.

- **Python Example**:

```python
Copy
import os
file_path          =
os.path.join("folder",
"file.txt")
```

- **C# Example**:

```csharp
Copy
using System.IO;
string          filePath          =
Path.Combine("folder",
"file.txt");
```

2. **Platform-Specific APIs**:

o **Issue**: Certain APIs or libraries may be platform-specific and may not be available on all platforms. For instance, using native system APIs

190

for networking or accessing hardware may work on one OS but fail on others.

o **Solution**: Use cross-platform libraries or check the platform at runtime to ensure compatibility. In Python, you can use libraries like `requests` for HTTP requests or `PyQt` for building GUIs that work across platforms. In C#, use the .NET Core framework, which provides many platform-agnostic APIs for networking, file handling, and more.

- **Python Example** (Using `requests` for HTTP requests):

```python
Copy
import requests
response =
requests.get("https://example
.com")
```

- **C# Example** (Using .NET Core APIs):

```csharp
Copy
using System.Net.Http;
HttpClient client = new
HttpClient();
```

191

```
HttpResponseMessage response =
await
client.GetAsync("https://exam
ple.com");
```

3. **UI and Layout Differences**:

   o **Issue**: The user interface (UI) of a cross-platform app may look and behave differently on each platform due to platform-specific design conventions and screen sizes.

   o **Solution**: Use responsive design techniques and layout libraries that adjust the UI based on screen size and platform. Xamarin provides **XAML** for building UI layouts that adapt to different platforms. In Python, you can use **PyQt** or **Kivy**, both of which provide layout management to handle different screen sizes.

   - **Xamarin Example** (Responsive UI with Xamarin.Forms):

   ```xml
   Copy
   <StackLayout>
       <Label Text="Hello, Cross-
   Platform!" />
       <Button Text="Click Me" />
   </StackLayout>
   ```

192

- **PyQt Example** (Responsive UI with PyQt):

```python
Copy
from PyQt5.QtWidgets import
QApplication, QLabel,
QPushButton, QVBoxLayout,
QWidget

app = QApplication([])
window = QWidget()

layout = QVBoxLayout()
layout.addWidget(QLabel("Hell
o, Cross-Platform!"))
layout.addWidget(QPushButton(
"Click Me"))

window.setLayout(layout)
window.show()
app.exec_()
```

4. **Library and Dependency Compatibility**:

   o **Issue**: Certain libraries or dependencies may not be available or behave differently on various platforms. For instance, a library that is optimized for Linux may not function the same way on macOS or Windows.

193

o **Solution**: Use libraries that are known to be cross-platform, and if necessary, use conditional imports or platform-specific implementations. In Python, `platform` and `sys` can be used to detect the operating system and conditionally load dependencies. In C#, use `#if` preprocessor directives to conditionally compile code based on the platform.

- **Python Example** (Using `platform` to handle platform-specific behavior):

```python
Copy
import platform

if platform.system() ==
"Windows":
    import
windows_specific_lib
elif platform.system() ==
"Linux":
    import linux_specific_lib
```

- **C# Example** (Using `#if` for platform-specific code):

```csharp
Copy
```

194

```
#if WINDOWS
    // Windows-specific code
#elif LINUX
    // Linux-specific code
#endif
```

5. **Performance Variations**:

   o **Issue**: Cross-platform apps may perform differently on different platforms due to variations in hardware, OS optimizations, and other factors.

   o **Solution**: Optimize your code for performance across platforms and test on various devices and operating systems. Use profiling tools to identify performance bottlenecks and address them. In Python, `cProfile` can help you profile code performance, while in C#, you can use Visual Studio's profiling tools to measure and optimize performance.

Debugging and Testing Strategies for Cross-Platform Compatibility

1. Automated Cross-Platform Testing:

- **Issue**: Manually testing your application on all target platforms can be time-consuming and error-prone.
- **Solution**: Implement automated testing for your cross-platform app using frameworks that support multiple

platforms. Tools like **Selenium** (for UI testing), **Appium** (for mobile testing), or **pytest** (for unit testing) can be integrated into your CI/CD pipeline to automate tests across various platforms.

- **Example** (Using Selenium for automated UI testing across platforms in Python):

```python
Copy
from selenium import webdriver

def test_login():
    driver = webdriver.Chrome()

driver.get("https://example.com/login")

driver.find_element_by_id("username").sen
d_keys("user")

driver.find_element_by_id("password").sen
d_keys("password")

driver.find_element_by_id("login_button")
.click()
    assert "Dashboard" in driver.title
    driver.quit()
```

2. Platform-Specific Debugging:

- **Issue**: Debugging cross-platform apps can be challenging, as issues might only occur on specific platforms.

- **Solution**: Use platform-specific debuggers and logs to diagnose issues. Both Python and C# offer powerful debugging tools, including integrated debuggers in IDEs like Visual Studio, PyCharm, or VS Code. Make use of detailed logs and error messages to trace platform-specific issues.

- **Python Debugging**:

  o Use the `pdb` module to set breakpoints and step through code to identify issues.

  o Example:

  ```python
  Copy
  import pdb
  pdb.set_trace()    # Execution will pause here
  ```

- **C# Debugging**:

  o Use Visual Studio's built-in debugger to step through code, set breakpoints, and inspect variables. You can also use logging to track the flow of execution and capture detailed information about platform-specific errors.

3. Cross-Platform Testing with Virtual Machines or Containers:

- **Issue**: Testing on physical devices or multiple operating systems can be resource-intensive.
- **Solution**: Use virtual machines (VMs) or containers to simulate different environments for testing your application. Tools like **Docker** can help containerize your app, making it easy to test it across different platforms without needing multiple physical devices.
- **Example**: Using Docker to test a cross-platform application:

```bash
Copy
docker build -t myapp .
docker run -p 5000:5000 myapp
```

Real-World Examples of Overcoming Compatibility Challenges

Example 1: Cross-Platform Mobile App (Xamarin):

- **Scenario**: A mobile app needs to work on both iOS and Android, but platform-specific issues are causing UI inconsistencies.
- **Solution**: The app uses Xamarin to create a single codebase. By using Xamarin.Forms for UI, the app's layout is designed to adapt to both platforms. Platform-

specific differences in UI design are handled using conditional code in the XAML files and C# code behind, ensuring that platform-specific controls are used where necessary.

- **Outcome**: The app works consistently on both iOS and Android, and any platform-specific adjustments are made using Xamarin's cross-platform capabilities.

Example 2: Cross-Platform Web App (Flask + Vue.js):

- **Scenario**: A web application built with Flask (Python) for the backend and Vue.js for the frontend faces issues with file handling and path management on different platforms.

- **Solution**: The Flask app uses the `os.path` module to handle file paths in a cross-platform way, and the Vue.js app is designed to adjust dynamically to different screen sizes and platforms using responsive design principles. Automated tests are set up using Selenium to test the web app across different browsers (Chrome, Firefox) and operating systems (Windows, macOS, Linux).

- **Outcome**: The application runs smoothly across all platforms and browsers, with no file path issues or UI inconsistencies.

Example 3: Cross-Platform Desktop App (Electron + Node.js):

- **Scenario**: A desktop app built with Electron needs to ensure that native components like file handling and notifications work correctly on macOS, Windows, and Linux.
- **Solution**: The app uses Electron's built-in APIs for accessing native features, and conditional logic is applied to handle platform-specific behavior. Automated testing is done using **Spectron**, which simulates user interaction with the Electron app and verifies cross-platform compatibility.
- **Outcome**: The app functions correctly on all supported operating systems, with platform-specific features working seamlessly.

In this chapter, we explored the common issues faced when developing cross-platform applications, including file system differences, platform-specific APIs, and UI inconsistencies. We also provided strategies for debugging and testing cross-platform compatibility, including using platform-agnostic libraries, debugging tools, and automated testing frameworks. Finally, we presented real-world examples demonstrating how to overcome these compatibility challenges, showing that with the right approach, cross-platform development can be both efficient and effective.

CHAPTER 18

ADVANCED INTEGRATION WITH LEGACY SYSTEMS

Integrating new cross-platform applications with existing legacy systems is one of the most complex and challenging tasks in enterprise software development. Legacy systems are often built using outdated technologies, and the architecture may not be conducive to modern practices like microservices, cloud computing, or agile development. However, the need for integration arises when businesses want to modernize their systems without completely overhauling their legacy infrastructure. In this chapter, we will explore strategies for integrating new cross-platform apps with legacy systems, the role of middleware and messaging queues in this integration, and provide examples of real-world enterprise solutions that successfully integrate legacy systems.

Integrating New Cross-Platform Apps with Existing Legacy Systems

Challenges in Legacy System Integration:

- **Outdated Technology**: Legacy systems are often built with older technologies that may not be compatible with modern programming languages, platforms, or protocols.
- **Data Incompatibility**: Legacy systems may use proprietary data formats or older database models that need to be transformed or migrated to work with new systems.
- **Limited APIs**: Many legacy systems lack proper APIs or use non-standard communication protocols, making integration more difficult.
- **Scalability Issues**: Legacy systems may struggle to handle modern demands, and integrating them with new applications can strain performance.

Strategies for Integration:

1. **Expose Legacy Functionality via APIs**:
   - One of the most common ways to integrate legacy systems with modern applications is to expose the functionality of the legacy system through APIs. For instance, you can create a RESTful API that wraps around the existing legacy application to provide modern, standardized access to its data and services.
   - **Example**: In a financial organization, a legacy system might be handling transactions, but the new mobile app needs access to that data. By

developing an API around the legacy system, you can provide real-time data access to the mobile application without modifying the core legacy system.

o Tools like **API gateways** (e.g., Kong, AWS API Gateway) can be used to manage API exposure and integrate legacy systems with newer microservices or cloud platforms.

2. **Data Synchronization and Transformation**:

   o In many cases, data structures in legacy systems may not align with those in the new applications. A **data transformation layer** is often necessary to translate data between formats (e.g., XML to JSON, or relational data to NoSQL formats).

   o **Example**: A legacy SQL database may use a different schema than a modern NoSQL database used by a cross-platform mobile app. Middleware solutions like **ETL (Extract, Transform, Load)** tools or custom adapters can be used to synchronize data between the old and new systems.

3. **Wrap Legacy Systems with Service-Oriented Architecture (SOA)**:

   o You can wrap legacy systems with **service-oriented architecture (SOA)**, allowing the legacy systems to communicate with modern applications via service interfaces. SOA breaks down functionality into smaller services that can be consumed by the new system, making it easier to integrate disparate systems.

- o **Example**: A company has an existing ERP system with proprietary functionality, but needs to integrate it with new cloud-based CRM and inventory systems. By exposing ERP functionalities through SOA, each service can be independently consumed by the new cloud applications, even if the legacy ERP system remains unchanged.

4. **Use of Middleware**:

- o Middleware solutions provide a layer between the legacy systems and new applications, facilitating communication between different technologies and platforms. Middleware acts as a bridge to ensure that different systems can exchange data and process requests efficiently.
- o Middleware is often used to abstract differences in technology stacks, manage message routing, and enable secure communication.
- o **Example**: Middleware like **IBM MQ** or **Tibco** can route messages between a legacy mainframe system and a cloud-based mobile app, providing

seamless communication without modifying either system.

Using Middleware and Messaging Queues

What is Middleware?

Middleware is software that connects different systems or applications, enabling them to communicate and share data. It sits between the operating system and the application software, managing communication between different components of an application or between applications themselves. Middleware plays a crucial role in bridging the gap between legacy systems and modern applications.

Types of Middleware for Integration:

1. **Message-Oriented Middleware (MOM)**:
   o **MOM** facilitates communication between applications using messages and message queues. It's especially useful for asynchronous communication in distributed systems, allowing systems to communicate in a decoupled and fault-tolerant manner.
   o Examples include **Apache Kafka**, **RabbitMQ**, **IBM MQ**, and **Azure Service Bus**.
2. **Database Middleware**:

206

o **Database middleware** connects applications to legacy databases that don't have modern API access. It can act as an abstraction layer to allow applications to read and write data to legacy systems without directly interacting with the database.

o Examples include **ODBC**, **JDBC**, and custom middleware that can convert legacy database queries into modern database protocols.

3. **Integration Middleware**:

o These tools help connect legacy systems with modern systems by handling communication, data transformation, and transaction management. Middleware like **MuleSoft** and **WSO2** can help in creating API-driven integration solutions that allow legacy systems to communicate with cloud or microservices architectures.

Using Messaging Queues for Legacy Integration: Messaging queues are used to pass messages between systems in an asynchronous manner. For legacy systems that cannot handle real-time communication or synchronous APIs, messaging queues provide an efficient way to enable communication without directly modifying the legacy system.

- **Example**: A legacy inventory management system may generate events whenever stock levels change, but it cannot handle modern RESTful API calls. A messaging queue (e.g., RabbitMQ) can be used to send messages from the legacy system to new cross-platform applications or microservices that subscribe to inventory events.

Example of Integration Using Middleware (Python + Legacy System):

- A financial services company wants to integrate a modern mobile app with a legacy mainframe system that handles transactions. Using **RabbitMQ** as a message queue, the mobile app can send messages to the middleware, which forwards them to the legacy system. The legacy system processes the transactions and sends the result back through the same messaging queue, which is picked up by the mobile app in real time.

```python
Copy
import pika

# Establish connection to RabbitMQ
connection = pika.BlockingConnection(pika.ConnectionParameters('localhost'))
```

```
channel = connection.channel()

# Sending message to the legacy system
channel.basic_publish(exchange='',

routing_key='legacy_queue',
                        body='Transaction  Request
Data')

# Receiving response from the legacy system
def callback(ch, method, properties, body):
    print(f"Received: {body}")

channel.basic_consume(queue='legacy_queue',
on_message_callback=callback, auto_ack=True)

channel.start_consuming()
```

Real-World Examples of Overcoming Compatibility Challenges

Example 1: Healthcare System Integration:

- **Scenario**: A healthcare company needs to integrate a new mobile app with an old hospital management system running on legacy mainframe technology. The mainframe handles patient records and appointments but lacks API support.

- **Solution**: Middleware is used to expose the mainframe system's functionality via SOAP web services. These services are consumed by the mobile app using a RESTful API exposed by a modern API gateway. Data synchronization is managed through **IBM MQ**, which handles message routing between the mainframe and the new mobile app.

- **Outcome**: The integration allows healthcare professionals to view patient data and appointment schedules in real time on their mobile devices, without changing the core mainframe system.

Example 2: Retail Platform Modernization:

- **Scenario**: A retail company has an old point-of-sale (POS) system that handles transactions, inventory, and customer data but wants to build a modern cloud-based analytics platform.

- **Solution**: The company uses **Apache Kafka** as a messaging queue to pass transaction and inventory data from the POS system to the cloud platform. Kafka acts as a buffer, ensuring that data is passed asynchronously and that the legacy system is not overwhelmed. The cloud-based system processes this data in real time for analytics and reporting.

- **Outcome**: The retail company can now analyze sales and inventory data from the POS system in near real-time, improving decision-making and inventory management without needing to overhaul the POS system.

Example 3: Banking System Integration:

- **Scenario**: A bank is transitioning from a legacy core banking system (CBS) to a new digital platform for customer engagement. The CBS, which processes transactions, does not have modern API support, but the bank needs to allow customers to access their data on mobile and web apps.
- **Solution**: The bank uses a combination of **MuleSoft** (for integration) and **RabbitMQ** (for message queuing) to connect the CBS with the new digital platform. A middleware layer is developed to abstract the legacy CBS and provide modern APIs for the mobile and web apps.
- **Outcome**: The bank can offer customers a modern, seamless experience while continuing to use the legacy CBS for transaction processing.

In this chapter, we explored the complexities and solutions for integrating cross-platform applications with legacy systems. We discussed the use of middleware and messaging queues to bridge the gap between modern and legacy systems, as well as provided real-world examples of enterprise solutions successfully overcoming legacy system integration challenges. By using these strategies, businesses can modernize their infrastructure and bring new capabilities to their legacy systems, ensuring smoother operations and a better user experience across platforms.

CHAPTER 19

FUTURE TRENDS IN CROSS-PLATFORM APPLICATION DEVELOPMENT

The landscape of cross-platform application development is evolving rapidly, with new tools, frameworks, and technologies reshaping the way developers build software. In this chapter, we will explore emerging tools and technologies, examine the growing influence of AI and machine learning in cross-platform development, and discuss the future of Python and C# in the enterprise landscape.

Emerging Tools, Frameworks, and Technologies

The rise of modern tools and frameworks has significantly improved the efficiency, scalability, and maintainability of cross-platform applications. Here are some of the most promising emerging technologies:

1. **Flutter:**

o **Overview**: Flutter, developed by Google, has quickly become one of the most popular frameworks for cross-platform mobile development. It allows developers to build natively compiled applications for mobile, web, and desktop from a single codebase.

o **Key Features**:

- Uses a single codebase for multiple platforms (iOS, Android, Web, and Desktop).

- Provides high-performance rendering through its Skia graphics engine.

- Rich set of pre-designed widgets that mimic native app behaviors.

o **Future Outlook**: Flutter is expected to continue gaining traction due to its strong ecosystem, backing by Google, and growing community. It's likely to be a strong competitor to React Native in the mobile app space.

2. **Electron**:

o **Overview**: Electron allows developers to build cross-platform desktop applications using web technologies (HTML, CSS, JavaScript). It's already widely used in applications like Visual Studio Code, Slack, and Discord.

o **Key Features**:

- Leverages web technologies for desktop application development.
- Allows the use of native APIs for deeper integration with desktop platforms.
- Cross-platform support for Windows, macOS, and Linux.

  o **Future Outlook**: With the continued growth of web-based technologies, Electron is expected to remain a popular choice for building desktop apps. However, developers may face performance challenges as Electron apps tend to be heavier compared to native apps.

3. **Xamarin and .NET MAUI (Multi-platform App UI)**:

   o **Overview**: Xamarin has been the go-to cross-platform solution for C# developers. Microsoft's latest offering, **.NET MAUI**, extends Xamarin's capabilities to a broader range of platforms (iOS, Android, Windows, and macOS).

   o **Key Features**:
- Unified API for building apps across multiple platforms.
- Leverages the power of C# and the .NET ecosystem.
- Seamless integration with cloud and enterprise systems using Azure.

- o **Future Outlook**: .NET MAUI, combined with the growth of the .NET ecosystem, positions C# as a dominant language for cross-platform development in the coming years. It's likely to grow in popularity, especially within enterprise environments already using .NET technologies.

4. **WebAssembly (Wasm)**:

- o **Overview**: WebAssembly is an emerging technology that enables high-performance execution of code in web browsers. Developers can write code in multiple languages (C, C++, Rust, etc.) and compile it to WebAssembly for efficient, platform-independent execution.
- o **Key Features**:
  - Supports languages like C, C++, Rust, and more in the browser.
  - Provides near-native performance for web applications.
  - Enables the development of cross-platform applications that run in web browsers, mobile apps, and even desktop environments.
- o **Future Outlook**: WebAssembly is expected to revolutionize web app development by allowing developers to use lower-level languages for better

216

performance, providing broader support for cross-platform web and desktop applications.

5. **Progressive Web Apps (PWAs)**:

- ○ **Overview**: PWAs are web applications that offer a native app-like experience across devices while being accessible through a web browser. They combine the best features of websites and mobile apps, offering offline functionality, push notifications, and device access.

- ○ **Key Features**:
  - Works on any device with a web browser.
  - Offers offline capabilities and push notifications.
  - Lightweight and fast, providing an app-like experience without needing to be downloaded from an app store.

- ○ **Future Outlook**: PWAs are gaining popularity, especially for companies looking to build apps that work seamlessly across devices without needing to develop native apps. They're poised to become the standard for mobile-first web experiences.

How AI and Machine Learning Are Influencing Cross-Platform Development

AI and machine learning (ML) are not only transforming how software is developed but also impacting the development and operation of cross-platform applications. Here's how:

1. **Automated Code Generation**:
   - o **AI-Powered IDEs**: Modern Integrated Development Environments (IDEs) powered by AI, like **GitHub Copilot**, are able to suggest and generate code based on the context of the developer's work. This can significantly speed up the development process for cross-platform apps by automating repetitive tasks and offering solutions for platform-specific code.
   - o **Machine Learning Models for Code**: AI tools are also being trained to understand and generate platform-agnostic code that works across different environments. These tools can suggest optimizations and improvements that can make the app perform better across various platforms.

2. **Personalized User Experiences**:
   - o AI and machine learning can help developers deliver personalized experiences in cross-

218

platform applications by using data to predict user preferences, actions, and needs. This is particularly useful for mobile apps, where behavior can be analyzed to offer tailored content, personalized notifications, and suggestions.

3. **Cross-Platform Performance Optimization**:

    o **AI-Driven Optimization**: Machine learning models are being employed to analyze app performance on different platforms and optimize performance dynamically. By collecting data on user behavior, app performance, and resource utilization, AI can help make real-time decisions about app behavior, such as adjusting graphics rendering or switching between native and cross-platform modes depending on the platform's capabilities.

4. **Testing and Debugging with AI**:

    o **AI-Powered Testing**: AI is revolutionizing testing for cross-platform apps by automating test case generation, bug detection, and even suggesting fixes. Tools powered by AI, such as **Test.ai** or **Applitools**, can run extensive tests across platforms and devices, identifying issues that would be difficult for humans to spot.

o **Predictive Maintenance**: Machine learning algorithms can predict potential failures or bugs before they become a problem, allowing developers to address issues proactively across platforms.

5. **Chatbots and Virtual Assistants**:

   o Cross-platform apps are increasingly integrating AI-driven chatbots and virtual assistants to improve user engagement. These assistants can work seamlessly across web, mobile, and desktop platforms, providing users with the same level of support on any device.

Future of Python and C# in the Enterprise Landscape

Both Python and C# are highly valued in enterprise software development, but their roles in cross-platform development are evolving. Here's a look at the future of both languages in enterprise environments:

Python:

- **Data Science and AI Integration**: Python is already a leading language for data science, machine learning, and AI development. As these fields grow, Python's role in cross-platform development will become even more important, especially in fields like predictive analytics, automation, and intelligent applications.

- **Integration with Cloud Services**: Python's compatibility with cloud platforms like AWS, Azure, and Google Cloud means it will continue to be a strong choice for cloud-based cross-platform applications, particularly in areas like serverless computing and microservices.

- **IoT and Embedded Systems**: Python is gaining traction in the Internet of Things (IoT) and embedded systems domains, with tools like **MicroPython** and **CircuitPython**. This trend is expected to continue as cross-platform development expands into new domains, such as smart devices and wearables.

C#:

- **.NET MAUI (Multi-platform App UI)**: The future of C# in cross-platform development lies in **.NET MAUI**, a unified framework that allows C# developers to build apps for Windows, macOS, iOS, and Android with a single codebase. As the ecosystem continues to mature, C# is expected to become an even more powerful choice for cross-platform development in the enterprise space.

- **Cloud and Microservices**: With its robust support for microservices and integration with Azure, C# will continue to be a popular choice for developing scalable enterprise applications in the cloud. **Azure Functions** and

221

Azure Logic Apps are helping cement C#'s place in the cloud-first enterprise landscape.

- **Game Development**: C# remains a dominant language in the game development industry, especially with the **Unity** game engine. As game development expands into mobile, VR, and AR, C# will continue to be a key player in the cross-platform development space for interactive experiences.

Conclusion

Cross-platform application development is evolving at a rapid pace, with emerging tools, frameworks, and technologies paving the way for more efficient, scalable, and high-performance apps. As AI and machine learning continue to influence the development process, we can expect smarter, more personalized, and optimized applications. Both Python and C# remain critical languages in the enterprise landscape, each carving out its space in the future of cross-platform development. Whether you're building mobile apps with Flutter, web apps with PWAs, or leveraging the cloud with .NET MAUI, the future of cross-platform development holds exciting possibilities for developers and businesses alike.

CHAPTER 20

FINAL THOUGHTS AND CASE STUDY

In this final chapter, we'll consolidate the concepts, tools, and strategies discussed throughout the book by diving into a comprehensive case study of an enterprise-grade solution built using Python and C#. We'll then highlight key takeaways and best practices, and provide resources for further learning and development to ensure you're equipped to tackle the challenges of cross-platform application development in the future.

A Comprehensive Case Study of an Enterprise-Grade Solution Built with Python and C#

Scenario: A multinational retail company has decided to build a new enterprise-grade cross-platform solution for managing its online store, inventory, and customer relationships. The company needs a solution that works seamlessly across web, mobile, and desktop platforms, with real-time synchronization of data and transactions.

Objective: Build a scalable, secure, and high-performance cross-platform solution using Python and C# to handle user interactions, data processing, inventory management, and sales transactions.

Solution Architecture:

- **Frontend**: The frontend of the application is built using **React** for the web and **Xamarin** for the mobile application (iOS and Android), allowing the company to share code between the platforms.
- **Backend**: The backend is divided into microservices, where Python handles data analytics, recommendation engines, and customer management, and C# handles order processing, inventory management, and payments.
- **API Layer**: RESTful APIs are used for communication between the frontend and backend. Python's **FastAPI** and C#'s **ASP.NET Core** expose these APIs to allow data exchange between services and the frontend.
- **Database**: A relational database (PostgreSQL) is used for managing transactional data, while a NoSQL database (MongoDB) is used for storing product information and customer preferences.
- **Cloud Infrastructure**: The solution is hosted on **Microsoft Azure**, utilizing services like Azure App

Service, Azure Functions (for serverless processing), and Azure SQL Database.

- **Messaging and Middleware**: **RabbitMQ** is used for messaging and event-driven communication between the microservices, ensuring loose coupling and scalability.

Key Components:

1. **User Authentication and Authorization**: A Python microservice is responsible for authenticating users via OAuth 2.0, while C# manages user roles and access control within the application.

2. **Order Processing**: The C# backend manages the processing of customer orders, inventory updates, and payment gateway integration.

3. **Data Analytics and Recommendations**: Python handles data analytics, utilizing machine learning models to recommend products based on user behavior and sales trends.

4. **Cross-Platform Mobile Application**: The mobile app is developed using Xamarin, sharing code between iOS and Android platforms, and communicates with the backend using RESTful APIs for real-time order updates, notifications, and product recommendations.

Challenges Encountered:

1. **Integration of Legacy Systems**: The company had legacy systems for inventory and sales management that had to be integrated with the new solution. This was handled by developing APIs around the legacy systems and using **middleware** to facilitate communication between them.

2. **Performance Optimization**: The application needed to handle high traffic volumes, especially during sales events. Python and C# were optimized by using **caching** (Redis) and **load balancing** across multiple cloud instances.

3. **Cross-Platform UI Consistency**: Ensuring that the UI was consistent across web, mobile, and desktop required careful design and testing. **Xamarin.Forms** and **React** components were used to create responsive UIs for each platform.

4. **Data Synchronization**: Real-time synchronization between mobile, web, and desktop applications was a challenge. This was addressed by using **web sockets** and **push notifications** for mobile apps to ensure that inventory and order data were always up-to-date.

Outcome:

- **Seamless User Experience**: Customers could interact with the platform from any device—mobile, web, or desktop—and have a consistent experience with real-time updates.

- **Scalable Architecture**: The microservices-based architecture allowed the company to scale different components independently, such as the order processing service during high-demand periods.

- **Data-Driven Insights**: The Python-based recommendation engine provided personalized product suggestions, increasing sales and customer engagement.

- **Cost Efficiency**: Hosting on Azure with scalable services like Azure Functions and Azure App Service helped the company reduce infrastructure costs while maintaining flexibility and performance.

Key Takeaways and Best Practices

1. **Embrace Cross-Platform Development Early**: Building with cross-platform tools (like Xamarin for mobile and React for web) saves time, reduces development costs, and ensures consistency across different platforms.

2. **Microservices for Scalability**: The adoption of a microservices architecture allowed each service to be developed, deployed, and scaled independently, offering flexibility and fault isolation. This is especially important for enterprise-grade

applications that need to handle different functionalities and services efficiently.

3. **Use of Asynchronous Messaging**: Using middleware and messaging queues like **RabbitMQ** ensured decoupling between services, enabling asynchronous communication and scalability across platforms.

4. **Performance Optimization**: Implementing caching (with **Redis**) and load balancing was crucial for handling high traffic volumes during peak periods, ensuring that the system remained performant and responsive.

5. **Data Consistency and Synchronization**: Real-time data synchronization across platforms was made possible with technologies like **web sockets** and **push notifications**, ensuring that inventory, orders, and user interactions were always updated.

6. **APIs as the Bridge**: Exposing legacy systems as **APIs** was a key strategy to integrate old and new systems. This approach allowed for gradual migration and avoided the need for a full system rewrite, making the transition smoother and more manageable.

7. **Automated Testing**: Continuous testing and integration, combined with automated end-to-end tests, ensured that the system was always in a deployable state and that issues were caught early.

Resources for Further Learning and Development

As you continue your journey in cross-platform application development, here are some resources that will help you dive deeper into the tools, frameworks, and best practices:

1. **Books**:
   - *"Cross-Platform Development with C# and .NET"* by Christian Nagel
   - *"Python for Data Analysis"* by Wes McKinney
   - *"Learning Xamarin. Forms"* by John M. Wargo (for mobile app development)
2. **Online Courses**:
   - **Coursera**: Courses on cross-platform app development, microservices, and cloud computing.
   - **Pluralsight**: In-depth courses on Xamarin, .NET Core, Python, and enterprise application architecture.
   - **Udemy**: Courses on React, Python, Xamarin, and building scalable enterprise solutions.

3. **Documentation**:

   o **Xamarin Documentation**: https://docs.microsoft.com/en-us/xamarin/

   o **ASP.NET Core Documentation**: https://docs.microsoft.com/en-us/aspnet/core/

   o **Python Official Docs**: https://docs.python.org/3/

   o **React Documentation**: https://reactjs.org/docs/getting-started.html

4. **Communities and Forums**:

   o **Stack Overflow**: Great for asking questions and learning from the community.

   o **GitHub**: Explore open-source projects and contribute to cross-platform development.

   o **Reddit (r/crossplatform)**: Engage with developers and discuss cross-platform development trends and challenges.

5. **Tools for Testing and CI/CD**:

   o **Jenkins**: https://www.jenkins.io/

   o **GitLab CI**: https://about.gitlab.com/stages-devops-lifecycle/continuous-integration/

   o **Selenium**: https://www.selenium.dev/documentation/en/

6. **Cloud Platforms**:

   o **Microsoft Azure**: https://azure.microsoft.com/

   o **Amazon Web Services (AWS)**: https://aws.amazon.com/

○ **Google Cloud**: https://cloud.google.com/

In this final chapter, we reflected on a comprehensive case study of an enterprise-grade cross-platform solution built using Python and C#. We outlined key takeaways and best practices from this project and provided a range of resources to further your development skills. The future of cross-platform development is bright, with continuous advancements in tools, frameworks, and technologies that make it easier than ever to build scalable, high-performance applications across multiple platforms. With the knowledge from this book and the resources provided, you're now equipped to tackle your own cross-platform development challenges in the enterprise space.

www.ingramcontent.com/pod-product-compliance
Lightning Source LLC
La Vergne TN
LVHW051322050326
832903LV00031B/3317